INDIA
MISINFORMED

INDIA MISINFORMED

The True Story

Edited by

Pratik Sinha, Dr Sumaiya Shaikh and
Arjun Sidharth

HarperCollins *Publishers* India

First published in India in 2019 by
HarperCollins *Publishers*
A-75, Sector 57, Noida, Uttar Pradesh 201301, India
www.harpercollins.co.in

2 4 6 8 10 9 7 5 3 1

P-ISBN: 978-93-5302-837-4
E-ISBN: 978-93-5302-838-1

Typeset in 11.5/15 Minion Pro at
Manipal Digital Systems, Manipal

Printed and bound at
Thomson Press (India) Ltd

CONTENTS

BUILDING BRAND MODI

PORTRAYING OPPOSITION PARTIES AS ANTI-HINDU

RAHUL GANDHI – THE FAVOURITE FOR TARGETED PROPAGANDA

PM MODI AND THE BJP TARGETED

OTHER TARGETED POLITICIANS

FALSE HISTORICAL CLAIMS

MALIGNING JAWAHARLAL NEHRU

MAINSTREAM MEDIA

TARGETING INDIVIDUALS

FAKE POLLS, FAKE LISTS, FAKE ACCOUNTS

OTHERS

SCIENCE

FOREWORD

Ravish Kumar

FAKE NEWS HAS RESULTED in people getting murdered. Using fake news, the 'enemy' is marked on the basis of community. Fake news was spread so that the feeling of insecurity vis-à-vis this enemy constantly rises. Supporters and sympathizers of political parties, who subscribe to a particular ideology were presented with another facet of this ideology, which, instead of altering their political views, only ended up strengthening it. Fake news weaponized these political supporters, to whom it was disseminated day and night. The result was that people began to be lynched on the streets. Once a mob gathers, it does not discern the 'enemy'. Pehlu Khan (Alwar murder, 2017) is killed and so is Subodh Kumar Singh (Bulandshahr murder, 2018). Often, after an incident of lynching, fake news was spread in such a manner, or the incident was reported in such a way, that everything began to seem fake, to the extent that viewers readers found the murders of Pehlu Khan and Subodh Kumar Singh fake as well.

यहां फ़ेक न्यूज़ के कारण लोगों की हत्याएं हुई हैं। फ़ेक न्यूज़ के ज़रिए मज़हब के आधार पर दुश्मन तय किया गया। उस दुश्मन से असुरक्षा बढ़ती जाए इसके लिए फ़ेक न्यूज़ फैलाया गया। विचारधारा से प्रभावित होकर किसी राजनीतिक दल

के करीब आने वाले समर्थकों को फ़ेक न्यूज़ के ज़रिए उसी रंग की एक दूसरी विचारधारा दी गई, जिससे उनकी राजनीतिक निष्ठा बदलने की जगह और गहरी हो जाती और उनका इस्तमाल हथियार के रूप में होने लगता। फ़ेक न्यूज़ ने उन राजनीतिक समर्थकों को हथियार के रूप में बदल दिया जिन तक दिन–रात तरह–तरह के ऐसे न्यूज़ पहुंचाए गए। नतीजाः सड़क पर लोग मारे जाने लगे। एक बार जब भीड़ बन जाती है तो उसे दुश्मन का रंग नज़र नहीं आता है। पहलू ख़ान भी मारा जाता है और सुबोध कुमार सिंह भी। कई बार हत्या के बाद जायज़ ठहराने के लिए फ़ेक न्यूज़ गढ़े गए या न्यूज़ को इस तरह कवर किया गया कि सब कुछ फ़ेक लगने लगे। यहां तक कि दर्शक और पाठक को पहलु ख़ान और सुबोध कुमार सिंह की हत्या भी फ़ेक लगने लगा।

In a democracy, flow of information keeps a citizen alert and sensitive. If this information is manipulated, it can deceive her/him and s/he can become cruel. Fake news helped create a climate of fear and stoked majoritarian sentiment. Those who are a part of this crowd realize that the number of those who think like them has increased. Through WhatsApp university and mainstream media, many forms of misinformation ended up gaining legitimacy. The responsibilty of the media was to set the record straight and place correct information before the people. However, media organizations either ignored the spectre of fake news or actively engaged in its dissemination.

Analysis of fake news reveals that much of it is related to spreading hate against the Muslim community. Earlier too, minorities were perceived in a certain manner by the majority community. Fake news has exacerbated this tendency.

लोकतंत्र में सूचनाएं नागरिक को संवेदनशील और सतर्क बनाती हैं। अगर यही सूचनाएं बदल दी जाएं तो नागरिक क्रूर और भ्रमित हो सकता है। फ़ेक न्यूज़ से लैस भीड़ भय का माहौल रचने लगी। इसके ज़रिए लोगों के बीच बहुसंख्यकवाद को और भी उग्र किया गया। इस भीड़ में शामिल लोगों को पता है कि उनकी तरह सोचने वाला समाज पहले से बड़ा हो चुका है। व्हाट्सएप यूनिवर्सिटी और मुख्य धारा की मीडिया के माध्यम से फ़ेक न्यूज़ के कई तरह के रूप वैधानिकता

पाने लगे। मीडिया का काम था इन झूठी ख़बरों को पकड़ कर लोगों के सामने सही सूचना रखना। मगर मुख्यधारा का मीडिया फ़ेक न्यूज़ के प्रति या तो उदासीन हो गया या फिर जानबूझ कर फैलाने भी लगा।

फ़ेक न्यूज़ का अध्ययन करने पर पता चल जाता है कि इसका एक बड़ा हिस्सा मुसलमानों के प्रति नफ़रत फ़ैलाने से जुड़ा है। पहले भी बहुसंख्यकों के बीच अल्पसंख्यक ख़ास नज़र से देखे जाते हैं, मगर अन्य(वजीमत) के रूप मे देखे जाने की इस प्रक्रिया को फ़ेक न्यूज़ ने कहीं ज़्यादा तेज़ कर दिया है।

An organized machinery has been put in place for dissemination of fake news. BJP President Amit Shah has already stated on record that during the elections that took place in Uttar Pradesh a year ago, BJP's social media workers made two big WhatsApp groups. One had fifteen lakh members, the other seventeen lakh. This means a total of thirty-two lakh. And every day at 8 a.m. they would send 'Know the Truth'. This way, stories about BJP were sent to the newspapers apparently through WhatsApp. They would even go viral at times.

Shah said, 'But we had a volunteer who was smart. He put a message in the group that Akhilesh Yadav had slapped Mulayam Singh. No such thing had happened. Mulayam and Akhilesh were 600 kilometres apart. But he put this message. And the social media team spread it. It spread everywhere. By 10 that day my phone started ringing – bhaisahab, did you know Akhilesh slapped Mulayam ... So, the message went viral. One should not do such things. But in a way he created a certain *mahaul* (perception). This is something worth doing but don't do it! (*Crowd laughs*) We can do good things too. We can deliver any message we want to the public, whether sweet or sour, true of fake. We can do this work only because we have thirty-two lakh people in our WhatsApp groups.' (translated)

This message was fake, but the president of a national party was referring to how it was utilized.

फ़ेक न्यूज़ को फैलाने के लिए पूरा तंत्र खड़ा किया जा चुका है। बीजेपी के राष्ट्रीय अध्यक्ष अमित शाह बोल चुके हैं कि उनके पास यूपी में 32 लाख व्हाट्सएप ग्रुप हैं। वे चाहें तो इसके ज़रिए झूठ भी फैला सकते हैं और सच भी। बेशक दूसरे दलों के फ़ेक न्यूज़ पकड़े गए हैं। अमित शाह ने शान से बताया कि कैसे यूपी चुनाव के समय मेसेज आया कि अखिलेश यादव ने मुलायम सिंह को चांटा मारा। उनके फोन पर भी यह मेसेज आया और देखते–देखते फैल गया। यह मेसेज ग़लत था यानी फ़ेक न्यूज़ था। मगर राष्ट्रीय पार्टी का अध्यक्ष बता रहा है कि कैसे उसका इस्तमाल किया गया। एक तरह से अमित शाह ने राजनीतिक लाभ मिलने की लड़ाई में फ़ेक न्यूज़ के इस्तमाल को जायज़ बता दिया।

I am saying this so that the extent and spread of the fake news ecosystem can be comprehended. It ought to have been by the media, but anchors and correspondents themselves have become the flag-bearers of fake news. Many chose to ignore fake news, in the belief that exposing it may result in angering the government. It is needless to state who is benefiting from fake news. At many places, riot-like situations have emerged due to fake news.

यह इसलिए बता रहा हूं ताकि पता चले कि फ़ेक न्यूज़ का साम्राज्य कितना बड़ा हो चुका है। कायदे से इस प्रति भारत के मीडिया को लगना चाहिए था मगर वे और उनके एंकर–संपादक खुद ही फ़ेक न्यूज़ के ध्वज–वाहक बन गए। बहुतों ने इस डर से फ़ेक न्यूज़ को अनदेखा कर दिया कि इसकी पोल खोलने का मतलब है सरकार की नाराज़गी मोल लेना। यह बताने की ज़रूरत नहीं है कि फ़ेक न्यूज़ से किसे राजनीतिक लाभ हो रहा था। कई जगहों पर फ़ेक न्यूज़ के कारण दंगों जैसी स्थिति बन गई। जनता ने सूझ–बूछ का परिचय न दिया होता तो आज हम फ़ेक न्यूज़ के और भी ख़तरनाक रूप देख रहे होते।

There is undoubtedly greater awareness now about fake news, but where did this all begin? Through the efforts of individuals like Pratik Sinha. There were others too but they could not hold on. Pratik Sinha, on the other hand, has given this fight an organizational form. He established Alt News, where fake news is busted every single day. Not only fake news from the BJP, but also from Congress supporters. Newspapers the world over were engaged in countering fake news but in India, this person was fighting alone. Today, Pratik has become a fact-checker for the media. Media has outsourced the fight against fake news.

बेशक अब फ़ेक न्यूज़ को लेकर जागरूकता बढ़ गई है लेकिन इसकी शुरूआत कैसे हुई? प्रतीक सिन्हा जैसे इंडिविजुअल्स के प्रयासों से। कुछ और लोग भी थे जो इस मैदान में टिक नहीं सके, मगर प्रतीक सिन्हा ने अपनी इस लड़ाई को संस्थागत रूप दे दिया। आल्ट न्यूज़ बनाई, जहां हर दिन किसी न किसी फ़ेक न्यूज़ की पहचान की जाती है। सिर्फ बीजेपी के फ़ेक न्यूज़ की ही नहीं, कांग्रेस के समर्थकों द्वारा फैलाए जा रहे फ़ेक न्यूज़ की भी। दुनिया भर के अख़बार फ़ेक न्यूज़ से लड़ रहे थे, भारत में यह शख्स अकेला लड़ रहा था। आज प्रतीक मीडिया के लिए फैक्ट–चेकर बन गए हैं। मीडिया को उसके टैग लाइन में भले ही सच से लड़ने के कई रूप मिल जाएंगे मगर फ़ेक न्यूज़ की लड़ाई उसने आउट सोर्स कर दी।

This book by Pratik Sinha is reaching you in the form of a document. Reading this will make one understand the games being played through the use of misinformation, and the organized entities behind them. The future of any democracy depends on the alertness of its citizens. Fake news has sought to replace this alacrity in a rather sly manner. The citizen was made to feel that he/she is loyal to the country, and that certain sections are not allowing the nation to progress. It is unfortunate that fake news is being used to intensify this feeling, so that you may end up supporting falsehood under the illusion that you are doing the right thing.

प्रतीक सिन्हा की यह किताब एक दस्तावेज़ के रूप में आपके हाथों में पहुंच रही है। इस किताब को पढ़ते हुए आप महसूस कर सकेंगे कि फ़ेक न्यूज़ के ज़रिए किस तरह का खेल खेला जा रहा था। इसके पीछे के संगठन की पहचान कर सकेंगे। दुनिया के किसी भी लोकतंत्र का भविष्य उसके नागरिकों की सतर्कता

पर निर्भर करता है। फ़ेक न्यूज़ के ज़रिए बड़ी चालाकी से नागरिकों की सतर्कता को रिप्लेस करने का प्रयास किया गया। उसे अहसास कराया गया कि वह अपने देश से प्यार कर रहा है। कुछ लोग देश को आगे नहीं बढ़ने दे रहे हैं। अफ़सोस कि उस अहसास को फ़ेक न्यूज़ से गढ़ा जा रहा था। ताकि आप ख़ुद को सही समझते हुए सामने के झूठ का समर्थन कर सकें।

The 'citizenry' of a citizen can be altered. The strength of democracy is the people to whom information is relayed. Is it possible that the information reaching them is manipulated, so that they may continue supporting democracy but the control over its institutions is in the hands of those who have cast a net of misinformation? The evaluation of any government must be done on the basis of the freedom of the media and its commitment to facts, during the government's rule. If that is not so, then citizens must begin by evaluating themselves, as to whether they truly are citizens or not. Please read this book, so that you realize what has been done to you, and what may happen further.

नागरिक के भीतर की नागरिकता बदली जा सकती है। जिन लोगों तक सूचनाएं पहुंचती हैं, वही लोग लोकतंत्र की ताकत हैं। क्या ऐसा हो सकता है कि उन लोगों तक पहुंचने वाली सूचनाएं बदल दी जाएं ताकि वे लोकतंत्र का समर्थन तो करते रहें मगर उसकी संस्थाओं पर कब्ज़ा ग़लत सूचनाओं का जाल फैलाने वालों का हो जाए? किसी भी सरकार का मूल्यांकन इस बात से शुरू होना चाहिए कि उसके दौर में मीडिया कितना स्वतंत्र है। तथ्यों के प्रति समर्पित है। अगर ऐसा नहीं है तो फिर नागरिकों को सरकार से पहले अपना मूल्यांकन करना चाहिए। यही कि वो नागरिक है भी या नहीं। आप इस किताब को पढ़ें, आपको पता चलेगा कि आपके साथ क्या हो रहा था। क्या हो सकता है।

Reference: https://thewire.in/politics/amit-shah-bjp-fake-social-media-messages

INTRODUCTION

Pratik Sinha

IN THE RUN-UP TO the 2014 general elections in India, an image[1] of a swanky bus stop was circulated claiming that it was the Bus Rapid Transport System from Ahmedabad. The objective of the tweet was to showcase the 'Gujarat Model' but in reality, the image was not from Ahmedabad, but from Guangzhou in China. The person who shared this image reportedly went on to hold an authoritative position in his new professional role after the 2014 elections. Today, the phrase 'fake news' is a commonly used one in most urban and semi-urban households. However, it is often said that the practice of using social media to mislead the populace at large for political propaganda had already begun in India in 2012-13.

In the month of August 2015, a website that displayed a strong affiliation to a certain religion was registered. The founder of this website put up a video in 2016 promoting blogging as a business idea. In this video, he claimed that his websites got twelve to fifteen million hits a month. This video also featured a screenshot of the owner's ad revenue, which would show an incremental increase every time someone clicked on one of the several ads embedded

[1] http://entecity.com/news/how-chinas-brts-landed-up-in-modis-gujarat/

embedded within the articles on the portal. In one of its articles, the portal had posted a video claiming that a man from a majority community was murdered by members of a minority community, and Indian media was silent about it. This was in the backdrop of a cattle trader, Pehlu Khan[2], being lynched in Alwar, Rajasthan. The video was actually from Bangladesh and had no element of inter-religious conflict. This owner of the portal seemed to have figured out two objectives in one go – political propaganda and financial gains.

The growth of such websites happened at the same time as when internet usage in India saw a steep rise. In June 2016, India as a country was reportedly using 200 million GB of data per month. By March 2017, this figure had increased to 1.3 billion – an increase of six and a half times in a space of nine months. Internet was now reaching the farthest corners of this country. Usually, such growth would bring unlimited cheer. After all, the Internet is an enormously empowering technology. However, while online websites providing door-to-door services and Internet banking services flourished, a tragedy struck in May 2017.

A picture of Mohammed Naeem[3], begging for his life with folded hands, his face dripping with blood, shirt ripped and his vest soaked in blood was splashed across several newspapers on 19 May 2017. Naeem, along with six other people, was lynched to death in Jharkhand after child kidnapping rumours went viral on WhatsApp. A Hindi text (translated) that was circulated via WhatsApp claimed, 'Suspected child lifters are carrying sedatives, injections, spray, cotton and small towels. They speak Hindi,

---

[2] https://www.nytimes.com/2017/04/05/world/asia/india-cow-mob-hindu-vigilantes.html

[3] https://www.hindustantimes.com/india-news/pictures-of-man-begging-for-life-become-defining-moment-for-jharkhand-killings/story-Q8Id5qIB24HGkBnrAKghNP.html

Bangla and Malayalam. If you happen to see any stranger near your house, immediately inform local police as he could be a member of the 'child-lifting gang'.

The fear of losing one's own child had caused people to come out on the street and lynch seven people, none of whom had committed any crime. Had internet come with a handbook, just the way the cooking stove in your home does, these seven people might have been alive today and over a dozen people would not have been jailed for the crime. What caused these murders? An absolute lack of Internet literacy.

A few months before these gruesome killings in Jharkhand, Alt News[4] was born in a room in Ahmedabad in February 2017 with the primary focus of fighting disinformation propagated in the Indian social media as well as the mainstream media ecosystem. One of our earliest fact-checks showed how a grisly video[5] of a young woman who was burnt alive for allegedly shooting a taxi driver in Guatemala was being circulated claiming her to be a Hindu Marwadi woman burnt in India by Muslims. Since then, we have penned over 1,000 articles and debunked and documented the most viral myths in India.

With a team that comprises talents from across various industries including technology, science, journalism, accounts, business and telecom, Alt News has debunked a wide range of myths. Among the present websites in India that are dedicated to the cause of fact-checking, Alt News attracts the most amount of web traffic. We publish in both English and Hindi, with the Hindi portal operational since April 2017. We operate under the aegis of a not-for-profit entity called Pravda Media Foundation.

---

[4] https://www.altnews.in/

[5] https://timesofindia.indiatimes.com/news/fake-alert-video-from-guatemala-shared-claiming-hindu-girl-was-burnt-alive-in-madhya-pradesh/articleshow/67122502.cms

In the past two years, certain clear patterns of misinformation have emerged. A prominent portion of this right-wing (RW) propaganda seems to be anchored around misinformation targeting minorities. From fake videos claiming that Muslims celebrated Pakistan's win over India in Champion's Trophy to falsely suggesting that the name of the driver of the ill-fated train that ran over several devotees on Dussehra in Amritsar was Imtiaz Ali, a concerted and organized attempt was being made to polarize by projecting minorities in a negative light and blaming them for real and imaginary crimes across the country.

The themes of nationalism also frequently surface in fake news stories in the form of rumours of Pakistan's flag being sighted or 'Pakistan Zindabad' slogans being heard in the rallies of political opponents of nationalist parties.

Distortion of history has also been a prominent theme. From pictures of Jawaharlal Nehru showing affection to his sister and niece shared as evidence of his 'character' to allegations that Indian football team had to play barefoot because of him, India's first prime minister remains one of the favourite targets of fake news.

Misinformation was also weaponized to target individuals such as journalists, activists, liberals and anyone who was critical of the right-wing ecosystem. Misinformation was also enthusiastically used to make misleading claims about the achievements of the union government. We saw fake endorsements of PM Modi by international leaders and a piece of misleading news about a Nobel laureate applauding demonetization.

In the first year, a large majority of misinformation came from the right-wing camp in India, but in the last twelve months, the non-RW political ecosystem has started to increasingly contribute to the spread of misinformation.

Misinformation peaks during certain times. Elections see a surge in false claims and accusations by rival political parties while any form of communal disturbance leads to fake news that seeks to further polarize communities. During the West Bengal riots, a still from a movie was widely circulated as a picture of a Hindu woman being molested by Muslims.

With multiple fact-checking websites working in tandem, prominent accounts on social media which had previously put out multiple instances of misinformation became vigilant. However, anonymous accounts started becoming the seeds of misinformation, especially on Twitter. At that same time, multiple Facebook pages came up and started churning out propaganda in a very professional manner which included quality infographics and videos. Alt News also discovered Facebook groups that were a dedicated marketplace for buying and selling of political Facebook pages. Themes such as the Indian Army, cricket players such as Virendra Sehwag, politicians such as Narendra Modi and Yogi Adityanath were seemingly common for these Facebook political pages. Quite a few of these pages had over a million followers and were apparently sold at hefty prices.

While misinformation was on the rise, instead of becoming allies, mainstream media became a part of the problem. While the misinformation on social media often comes from a position of malice, misreports in mainstream media was as if a function of the business model adopted by several Indian media outlets. Thanks to tight deadlines with pressures of producing unending content for web portals and 24x7 TV channels, fact-checking was done away with.

The most disturbing trend in this rise of fake news is the patronage it receives from political parties. Fake news doesn't exist in a vacuum. To thrive, it needs support not just from those who fall for it but also from those who benefit the most from it. Several Twitter users who routinely spread misinformation are followed by union ministers and in many cases, even the prime minister of the country seems to be doing so. Many of them proudly display their pictures with the leaders on their profiles. If misinformation continues to get political patronage, the fake news ecosystem will continue to flourish.

Apart from politically motivated misinformation, messaging and social media platforms are also flooded with misinformation about medicine, health and science. Alt News started its science fact-check section in April 2017. Since then, we have focused on fact-checking medical misinformation that is circulated in various forms, from misleading alternative medicine therapies to pseudo-scientific assertions. The 'Preface to the Science Section' will throw more light on this effort.

The sample messages used in this book are produced in order to cite examples of how fake news is circulated. The facts mentioned here intend to critique and initiate an important discourse on the harms of presumably accepting available information. This anthology is compiled without any intention of malice or harm. We hope readers will be discerning and refrain from misusing the information available in this book.

This book is an attempt to bring together prominent examples of misinformation that were circulated in the past two years.

PREFACE TO THE SCIENCE SECTION

Dr Sumaiya Shaikh

AS SOCIAL MEDIA HAS taken over print media as the preferred method of news consumption, the issue of misinformation has been given much attention. Misinformation, or 'fake news' as the media landscape has popularly labelled, is spread to successfully manipulate powerful narratives that impact politics, society, education, social structures and democracies. With the introduction of interactive media and the ability to form 'closed-groups' within social media platforms, users can choose to sever themselves off from those opinions that do not overlap with their own. This group-ism becomes tighter at each instant that further threatens their existing belief systems. As a result, the reinforcement of ideas in such online cocoons become impenetrable for various contradictory views.

Hitherto, this story-telling using manipulated narratives was used often to inject interpretive bias or a 'spin' to the existing process of knowledge production, and consumers of information were sometimes made aware to exercise caution while approaching such narratives. In India, Alt News has successfully helped clarify not only such befogged political narratives but also those that are concocted to typecast various community groups.

However, the fabrication of such narratives is seldom limited to achieve short to long term gains in politics. Akin to other parts of the world, in India, these narratives have branched into areas such as health and science, that directly threaten people's intellectual quotient as well as pose serious risks to their lives. Hence, medical information, if not wholly false or as popularly known as 'fake news', can include either concocted disinformation, one with falsely interpreted data of previously established evidence, or spread deliberately to harm an individual or a community. Together, we call it health misinformation.

According to the World Health Organization (WHO), misinformation in health, such as hesitancy to receive vaccines, has become a top global health concern[1]. Earlier in North America[2] and recently, in Europe[3], misinformation in the health and science category has directly threatened public health and scientific temperament. In both continents, a new era of epidemics arising from misinformation is causing the rise of what is now called '*misinfodemics*'.[4]

This misinformation in the west is not limited to an ostensible anti-vaccine movement, and the climate-change denial movement together called 'the snake-oil salesmanship,' but stretches beyond where scientific evidence is falsely represented to suit political agenda or increase the market of a specific novel alternative drug or therapy sold by dubious retailers.

At Alt News Science, the misinformation of this particular array of the health and sciences is debunked using technical skills based on years of scientific training, research and communication. Not only are we India's first in separating the wheat from the chaff, i.e. science from pseudoscience, but we have also done so without any bias towards of political, social or industrial organizations. As a result, one of the biggest challenges is identifying the threshold at which an intervention is required, that can diminish the adverse consequences related to the misinformation. For instance, providing a fact-check on misinformation that is not so viral can make it viral if written about, because of its ability to produce mass-fear. Secondly, due to limited resources, fact-checks in science are considered on the basis of its negative impact factor. While every type of misinformation causes harm in different ways, information that has immediate implications of life endangerment, e.g. vaccine-related, is given priority over those with low negative impact, i.e. consuming specific herbs to treat a common cold.

Furthermore, the scientific discourse taken during our Alt News Science research and presentation is of a kind that includes all the nuances of the misinformation. In contrast with political misinformation, our fact-checks for medical information with its technical complexities often doesn't end with overtly facile conclusions[5]. Of course, exceptions remain in cases of anti-vaccination rumours[6] and homeopathy treatments[7]. Secondly, with all its scientific references, the course, as well as the rationale of the research elaborated, our stories urge the readers to engage in the process that may allow them to conduct there in future. Thereby, encouraging readers to engage in self-driven research for their scientific questions, and, if required, can help educate themselves on some of the basic scientific misinformation being circulated. This form of citizen fact-checking can inject increased rationality and vigilance which is one of the most critical processes in curbing large volumes of misinformation.

Despite limited but basic scientific literacy, people have access to scientific literature on the internet such as through PUBMED and Google Scholar. However, to initiate peer-to-peer fact-checking such among friends or family directly or in WhatsApp groups, one must understand key characteristics of health misinformation and the types of people who believe in them.

Receiving a WhatsApp text or a video, scrolling through one's Facebook or Twitter timeline are one of the many examples of how individuals can be exposed to unverified content. While medical misinformation uses the same social media platforms and methods of outreach, the causes of virality here are significantly different. For other kinds of misinformation, fake news generators often understand the economic or political lucrativeness, and the pathology of the widespread damage it can cause. Their 'amplifiers' do not concoct the false narrative but strongly believe in it, and share it from their platforms. In stark contrast, except for most alternative treatment businesses, medical misinformation is shared or generated with the consideration that it will be beneficial as an effective or preventative treatment. Subsequently, sharing such advice increases the moral quotient, but in reality, disadvantages the receiver in the process.

Hence, at least in India, purveyors of medical misinformation condense down to four main brackets. These may not be precise categories and may often overlap. However, in an attempt to curb the damage propagated by medical misinformation, it is imperative to understand these actors that may cause its virality.

One, the wellness industry giants, alternative medicine (alt-med) practitioners and spiritual gurus, individuals from the government or government organizations such as the Ministry of AYUSH in India.

Outside of India, several food-industry 'critics' and 'wellness experts' such as the owner of FoodBabe by Vani Hari, and the lifestyle portal Goop by Gwyneth Paltrow that scream labels such as 'chemicals', 'harmful' and 'toxic' at every most consumable food available at the supermarket and only suggest those that are organic and non-genetically modified (non-GMO) to be safe. Needless to suggest, that their product inventory ranges from juice cleanses, detox diet plans, vitamin supplements, herbal drugs to even a straw embedded with a crystal rose quartz 'to radiate a heart-opening, calming vibe'.

In India, the manufacturers of wellness 'herbal' products have created a giant industry. Despite that, these industries sell other lifestyle products such as toiletries or groceries that work perfectly well as their ascribed basic function, some of the products labelled as 'medicine' have been produced with scant scientific evidence for efficacy. But more harmful are those individuals who are authorized by the government that spread health misinformation on social media as well as on their websites. Several treatments emerging as alternative medicine (alt-med) under the Ministry of AYUSH have been found to with scant research that has been largely ineffective[8,9]. Moreover, social media handles of government organizations such as the health ministry have also made misinformed statements related to diet and mental health[10].

Since these government organizations and large-scale companies have a huge advertisement budget and a relatively higher influence on the average population, any ill-researched treatment or misinformed health advice emerging from them can pose a mass-scale public health risk.

Two, the 'amplifiers' such as social media influencers with 'the good intent' of spreading the knowledge of 'cheaper and effective treatment'.

With the increasing omniscience and accessibility of internet tools and social media applications, a significant number of people are using them for researching medical information online. Online searches for common health symptoms in attempts to self-diagnose, or diagnose for someone else, often lead to results in searches that convince them of their condition being rare and non-curable, with the worst possible outcome or, at the very least detrimental. Also, when the online medical diagnostic search is used to determine the worst possible outcome for the patient concerned, it can add to the worst fears for both the patient and the caregiver.

Such individuals, without any former biological or clinical expertise, identify themselves as 'adequately knowledgeable' in the area of the given health issue by conducting a few hours of medical research, and often debate with experts with years of technical training on social media platforms 'to prove them wrong'. With exaggerated statements for or against a specific health issue, these 'amplifiers' often come with large social media following or a widespread network giving access to thousands of individuals at any given time.

This group is the most gullible to conspiracy theories ranging from anti-vaccine, big pharmaceutical industries to the dangers of consuming genetically modified products. They are often the hardest to rationalize using scientific data, as their belief system is robust, comes with good intent, somewhat modernized and skilled with using the internet and social media but with none or little understanding of scientific methods. With the rise in anti-vaccine content in India and abroad, mothers of young children are most susceptible and are the major role players in the creation and circulation of such information.

The content that targets people like them is simplified with occasional scientific jargon to maintain their existing beliefs, often involves a conspiracy theory or two about the health industry concealing a simple, yet an effective cure for a chronic ailment.

Hence, unlike the wellness giants or government organizations, they do not have the tools to advertise their belief but use social media to propagate misinformation at a relatively higher pace than most other individuals.

Three, the concerned relative of a sick or a vulnerable individual.

In consonance, with self-driven internet research in the health and sciences, there is a large number of gullible, naive and often low-resourced audience that will allow themselves to be convinced, that a non-toxic, cheaper alternative to cure obesity, autism or cancer can be attained by using the 'ingredients found in your kitchen.'

When the information circulated has successfully convinced people, they become habituated to share it further with those they are concerned about. These 'shares' are often limited to groups of 10s or 100s. Not doing so, may cause great self-doubt in the good intents of the person who had received it initially. This moral dilemma of 'sharing' or 'not-sharing' information with others on social media, that is exclusive and rare and possibly life-saving to the relevant individual, induces a great deal of cognitive reward. Such information that evokes an emotional response by nature comes with an information exclusivity and moral responsibility. This rewards often feed into conspiracies that may seem plausible as they allude to a beneficiary group or industry that wants to keep it from the consumers who need it the most for monetary gains. The people who share it also feel that their moral, social responsibility is complete by sharing the information to the people concerned and thus feel a rush of dopamine – the rewarding rush of neurotransmitter release in the brain cells that mimic the action of the brain under 'addictive' drugs.

This shared content across social media applications may become 'viral' and be passed off as a convincing piece of evidence generated by investing a few hours of internet search, despite seeming dubious and unverified by an expert in the field. It is this content that may be amplified later by category two of social media influencers.

This category is of utmost importance in convincing people with scientific evidence. Since, this category may comprise your inner circle of family and friends, trust and direct engagement is of utmost value. Acknowledging and addressing their concerns first can lead to exclusive trust and understanding of why they believe the misinformation in the first place.

Four, those with national and political interests who want to reiterate the merit of Ayurveda, Yoga or other ancient traditions but have a negligible understanding or research practices or medical science.

These often consist of politicians, celebrities or people without prominence, with 'ultra-nationalist' or 'far-right' views. Their belief, often blind, consists of attributing an immaculate status to ancient treatment methods, that are considered immune from any critique. By imparting greater importance to ancient scriptures, they are used to maintain an intellectual and ethnic superiority of the religious far-right in India. It has been given more legitimacy following 2014, where the department of AYUSH became an independent ministry.

In India, ridiculous scientific statements on genetics, evolution, organ transplant surgery and flight technologies are made to ascertain proof of evidence for mythological stories. In particular, the God-like status given to the bovine species is discussed extensively beyond health and sciences. Broadly, far-righters of every religion have a problem with 'fact- fullness' but some people learn to compartmentalize 'facts' used in everyday public life, from 'belief' used in everyday private life. In the event when this compartmentalization fails, what emerges are groups of people that hold extreme political and religious views that dictate the scientific path of a country, specifically in countries with authoritarian leaders like the US and Saudi Arabia. Here, overpowering misinformation in sciences, is used to justify not only politics, but also climate policy, energy use and women's lack of rights.

Although this is a new phenomenon in India, science has been misused by far-righters elsewhere as another political tool – from the theory of eugenics[11], Hans Asperger's clinical observations[12], to the recent actions of the 'alt-right' group in the US[13]. With the latter, a group of American Neo-Nazis also known as the 'alt-right' embraced milk as a symbol, to convey white supremacy. These protestors chugged entire cartons of milk in front of an anti-Trump protest, as a spectacle of proof that racial 'whiteness' makes someone biologically incapable of developing a lactose tolerance, hence suggesting racial superiority. The group misused and misinterpreted genetic research in profiling the human genome and evolutionary biology to arrive at such absurd conclusions. Although accounts of such incidents are incomparable with the supremacy derived from ancient scriptures, it is conclusive of the fact that political extremists have little to do with unbiased scientific evidence.

As a scientist trained in the west, it is my personal experience that this group is the hardest to convince as they are the ones most likely to dismiss any opinion enveloped with criticism. This group has its own set of conspiracy theories about people critical of the alt-med, often labelling us as 'brainwashed by modern training' or 'an agent of the drug mafia'.

Although the four categories as mentioned earlier may be ostensibly distinct, they operate with the common fear of ill-health and the ease of reproducibility of this fear in people. Since ill-health is a universal agony, the success of mass-reach of information based on such fear is understood. They can successfully use health misinformation to evoke mass-fear disguised as a word of caution to protect those around them. Also, since spreading such misinformation creates negative labels for big pharmaceuticals or health workers, sound scientific studies and genuinely hard-working health-care providers face massive threats that undermine their efforts.

Hence, strategies to combat such misinformation should also be well thought and devoid of emotional or political debates, largely to appreciate that most individuals debating for the potential therapies in alt-med may be doing so out of fear or moral compulsiveness. Although not always, in being clinical about the misinformation presented, one can somewhat combat the misjudgment of the individual arguing for the misinformation. It is not that that individual has no belief in science, but they are often cherry-picking the science to suit their belief systems. Hence, using a condescending tone may not be an effective strategy to convince them. Then, one may identify the parts of misinformation that have caused the most amount of agitation to address the specific fear of the individual. Later, the information can be broken down to identify the most illogical parts addressing their fears one by one. Thereafter, with an empathetic overtone, simplified and stark logical information can be delivered that has both expert advice and scientific evidence from published studies.

As previously suggested, medical misinformation has a more substantial impact on our society that wings beyond the manipulation of long-term political narratives. It has an immediate effect with severe risks to public health, or as a Duke University physician said, 'Medical misinformation might have even a greater body count.'[14] With the sheer volume of medical misinformation around us, the weight of this responsibility on a few individuals is too heavy a burden. With this seriousness, I am hopeful that more individuals, especially those who are experts in the area of the misinformation being circulated take active steps to curb the epidemic.

SPREADING COMMUNAL DISCORD

A CONVENIENT MEDIUM FOR purveyors of misinformation, social media has been weaponized in recent times with the objective of sowing the seeds of division, prejudice and hate among religious communities. The intention is, quite clearly, political gain. A systematic, synchronized and organized attempt is underway to paint the majority Hindu community as a victim of aggression by religious minorities on a daily basis. This is achieved through provocative messages that are shared on social media along with unrelated and disturbing pictures and/or videos.

This kind of messaging follows an established and predictable pattern – to show how Hindus are being oppressed in their own land by Muslims and Christians. Both these communities are painted as criminal and morally bankrupt. Over time, the nature, tone and content of these messages have become more vicious. Those who indulge in this kind of misinformation are constantly improvising, devising new tactics to create suspicion and fear.

This section highlights how this vicious cycle of hatred is generated and perpetuated.

1

AMRITSAR TRAIN ACCIDENT BLAMED ON 'TRAIN JIHAD' BY A MUSLIM DRIVER

IN OCTOBER 2018, MORE than sixty people lost their lives in a tragic accident where an Amritsar-bound train mowed down Dussehra revellers watching the burning of a Ravan effigy while standing on railway tracks. The tragic incident became an opportunity for communal rumour-mongering on social media by vested interests. Since the incident occurred in a Congress-ruled state, attempts were also made to link the incident to the party.

Claim: This was not an accident but a deliberate act of 'train jihad' carried out by a Muslim. The name of the train driver was Imtiaz Ali. Messages worded in venomous and communal language with a clear objective to incite hate were circulated. One tweet even wondered why trains do not run over people doing namaz.

Sample messages: *'Did anyone try to find out the religion of the train driver? Imtiaz Ali. Now you understand why the train did not stop and why the train was going at such a speed.'*

3

'*The name of the driver who killed over 250 was Imtiaz Khan. Rest you should be smart enough to know. This is not an accident but a planned mass murder.*'

'*We hear that the driver's name was Imtiaz Ali. Before this train, two other trains passed without any incident. We have never seen trains run over people doing namaz. If this is true, it should be investigated.*'

Incident: Alt News found evidence of an organized social media campaign where the same message was copy-pasted by several handles.

The handles behind these tweets had a common pattern that displayed strong political inclinations. A few handles were said to be followed by top right-wing leaders. Some of these tweets were also tweeted by self-proclaimed IT cell workers who happened to be followed by BJP leaders. A few handles followed by Prime Minister Narendra Modi also tweeted the claim.

Fact: A report on the accident written and signed by the train driver was shared by Indian news agency ANI. It revealed that the name of the driver involved in the Amritsar tragedy was Arvind Kumar.

Even after the actual name of the driver became public and was reported by media organizations, several social media users who had circulated this false, malicious information did not bother to delete their posts or acknowledge their mistake.

2

GRUESOME DETAILS OF ASSAULT ON PARESH MESTA

COMMUNAL VIOLENCE ERUPTED IN Karnataka towards the end of 2017, when inter-community clashes rocked the Uttara Kannada district. The decomposed body of twenty-one-year-old Paresh Mesta was found in a lake in Honnavar town, days after he had gone missing following communal clashes in the region. A picture of his body was used to claim torture and mutilation, and the mob which had gathered to protest his alleged murder turned violent, destroying vehicles and resorting to stone pelting.

Claim: A Bharatiya Janata Party (BJP) member of Parliament (MP) from Karnataka, Shobha Karandlaje, had alleged that Mesta had been brutalized and killed by 'jihadi elements'. What caused greater consternation was the tendency of the media to sensationalize the reporting around the incident. India Today broadcast a prime-time show on 11 December 2018 at 5.30 p.m. in which it reported gruesome details of the 'assault', claiming that Mesta had been castrated and his head split open, and that boiling oil had been poured on him.

This claim was also made by Mahesh Vikram Hegde, the founder of Postcard News.

Fact: The claim was false.

The Karnataka police released the following document from the department of forensic medicine in Manipal, which conducted the autopsy of Paresh Mesta. According to this document,

1. There was no evidence of injuries caused by weapons on the body of the deceased.

2. The change in the colour of the face of the deceased was due to putrefaction.

3. There was no evidence of castration or mutilation.

Alt News spoke to Inspector General (IG) of Western Range Hemant Nimbalkar who told us, 'There is a deliberate attempt to create [a] divide in society by circulation of false news as well as rumours through press notes, social media and particularly WhatsApp for personal gain. We are booking all those people who are trying to circulate false news and rumours through social media and already twenty cases are booked. Anybody who is abetting or circulating false news without authentication shall have to face the law.'

Reference: https://www.dailyo.in/voices/paresh-mesta-murder-karnataka-video-india-today-shiv-aroor-siddaramaiah-bjp/story/1/21141.html
https://www.thenewsminute.com/article/bjp-mp-shobha-karandlaje-booked-cops-spreading-communal-hatred-thru-tweets-73596

3

IMAGES OF HINDUS UNDER ATTACK IN BASIRHAT RIOTS, 2017

IN JULY 2017, COMMUNAL violence broke out at Basirhat in West Bengal. The situation on the ground was fanned by the flames of communalism as a flurry of inflammatory content was circulated on WhatsApp and social media platforms. This inciteful content was mainly in the form of Photoshopped images and tried to paint the state government in a negative light by accusing it of 'discriminating against Hindus'. Here are a few instances:

'WOMEN MOLESTED IN BROAD DAYLIGHT'

Claim: *'In Baduria, Hindu women are getting molested. Hindus who are still supporting TMC [Trinamool Congress], are you Hindu? If you are born of a Hindu father, then you will roar against these radicals. All Hindus of West Bengal must unite.'*

'Aparna Sen, where are you now? Peaceful people (read Muslims) are stripping Hindu women at Baduria.'

These messages were posted on Facebook, along with an image of a woman in a saree being stripped and harassed in broad daylight. Among those who shared the photograph was Vijeta Malik, a BJP office-bearer who alleged that Hindu women were facing harassment in West Bengal.

Fact: The still is from a Bhojpuri movie, *Aurat Khilona Nahin*, released in 2014.

Reference: https://www.ndtv.com/india-news/man-arrested-for-sharing-bhojpuri-film-still-as-image-of-bengal-violence-1722315
https://www.thecitizen.in/index.php/en/NewsDetail/index/2/11187/This-Is-How-Hate-and-Violence-is-Being-Generated-From-Muzaffarnagar-to-Basirhat
https://www.indiatoday.in/fyi/story/bjp-haryana-vijeta-malik-manoj-tiwari-bhojpuri-film-1022984-2017-07-07

4

'HINDU FAMILY ATTACKED'

A PHOTOGRAPH WAS SHARED on social media with the hashtag #HinduLivesMatter. The photo showed a man and a woman injured and bleeding, with the message, 'Souvik's parents. Attacked with no fault of their's [sic]. But they do not fall under the #NotInMyName narrative. #HinduLivesMatter.'

Gita S. Kapoor
@GitaSKapoor

Follow ⌄

Souvik's parents. Attacked with no fault of their's. But they do not fall under the #NotInMyName narrative. #HinduLivesMatter

9:35 PM - 6 Jul 2017

329 Retweets **169** Likes

Fact: The identical image was circulated during the 2016 Dhulagarh riots with the same claim – a Hindu family was attacked. The image is originally from Bangladesh where a Hindu family was assaulted.

The photo seems to have been sourced from Eibela, which is a Bangladeshi news site.

5

HINDU MAN LYNCHED BY MUSLIMS IN WEST BENGAL

Claim: A Twitter user whose handle was 'Jai Shri Ram' shared an image of a man called Karthik Gosh, 'lunched [sic] by Muslims in Basirhat'.

Fact: This was an unrelated image of a person by the name of Kartik Chandra Mete, shared by Hindutva websites in 2014. He was murdered in Falta, South Parganas, in West Bengal. According to a report, the murder had been solved in 2014 with the arrest of five people.

Reference: https://timesofindia.indiatimes.com/city/kolkata/CCTV-footage-solves-murder/articleshow/33042719.cms

6

'THIS IS A VICTORY OF ALLAH AND DEFEAT OF RAM'

IN MAY 2018, THE ruling BJP Party suffered a setback in the by-elections to the Lok Sabha seats of Gorakhpur, Phulpur and Kairana in Uttar Pradesh. In the aftermath of the verdict, a fake communally provocative quote attributed to a victorious candidate belonging to the Rashtriya Lok Dal (RLD) Party was circulated widely.

Claim: A provocative statement, 'This is the victory of Allah and defeat of Ram' was ascribed to Begum Tabassum Hasan, who won the Lok Sabha bypoll at Kairana. This quote began to circulate on social media almost immediately after the poll verdict.

Popular pages/accounts/handles which were believed to have shared it included: (on Facebook) Kamal Tyagi, BJP (who later deleted it), We Support Yogi Adityanath etc.

Fact: It was a fake quote, like several others which pepper the social media ecosystem on a daily basis. Begum Tabassum Hasan had never made this statement. This was confirmed by her in a conversation with Alt News. The damage, however, was done as thousands of people shared it across Facebook, Twitter and WhatsApp.

References: https://www.boomlive.in/will-file-fir-kairana-mp-tabassum-hasan-on-fake-quote-rld-blames-bjp/
https://www.facebook.com/WeSupportYogiAdityanathJi/photos/a.1753979107 949405/2434248056589170/?type=3

7

NEWSPAPER HEADLINE: HINDU GIRL STABBED TO DEATH BY MUSLIM MAN

Claim: *The Times of India* published an article titled, 'Hindu girl stabbed to death by Muslim man'. It should be noted that the newspaper later clarified that their article headline was tampered with using Photoshop on Twitter.

This was shared by Pratap Simha, a BJP MP , which he later deleted.

Fact: The image of *The Times of India* article was Photoshopped.

The original headline of the article read, 'Day after being stabbed by stalker, 21-year-old dies'.

The newspaper clip was Photoshopped and the title was changed. *The Times of India* clarified via a tweet that the image had been manipulated, adding that it would take legal action on the matter.

Reference: https://thewire.in/politics/bjp-fake-news-nupur-sharma

8

TEMPLE DISCOVERED UPON DEMOLITION OF A MOSQUE IN KARNATAKA

THE NARRATIVE THAT MODERN-DAY mosques which sit on modern day sites have been built on the ruins of temples demolished for the purpose has been one of the defining elements of politics in modern India, as evinced by the Babri Masjid-Ram Janmabhoomi episode. This narrative continues to play out on social media through the use of false photographs and accompanying claims.

Claim: Temple discovered upon demolition of a mosque in Karnataka.

'When a mosque was demolished in Raichur in Karnataka for widening road they have found the this temple. We need to demolish all mosques.' [sic]

This message was shared by social media users who posted it along with a photograph depicting what looked like a temple carved out of rock on Facebook and Twitter.

Fact: The photograph was a digital creation. Alt News fact-checked this claim and found that the image that was being circulated, claiming that to be of a temple found upon demolition of a mosque, is actually a digital creation by an artist. At the bottom right of the image, a logo with the text *'Chandra Colourist'* can be seen. We found a Facebook account named Chandra Colourist, which had posted the same image on 8 May 2016.

A photo of stone Buddhas from the Fengxiang temple in Luoyang, Henan, China, was used as the base image for this.

Reference: https://factcheck.afp.com/no-not-hindu-temple-discovered-after-mosque-was-demolished-india

9

INFLUX OF 11 CRORE ROHINGYAS AND 8 CRORE BANGLADESHI ILLEGAL IMMIGRANTS IN INDIA

MISINFORMATION REGARDING REFUGEES IN India is commonplace on social media. Their numbers are often inflated to generate panic. The Rohingya crisis and the ensuing refugee influx has not only led to divided opinion but also a divisive attempt to raise the spectre of demographic aggression. Moreover, the issue of illegal immigration from Bangladesh has always been a popular theme in Indian politics, with hatemongers and sources of false information seizing every opportunity to inflate the number of illegal immigrants.

Claim: The population of Rohingyas in India has risen to eleven crore. Also, there are eight crore Bangladeshis in India living illegally.

Sample messages: *The price of diesel, petrol increased by ₹5 and you declared Bharat bandh. But are those eight crore Bangladeshi and Rohingyas your family members that you support them? Hypocritical congressis. [sic]*

Fact: The numbers are totally off the mark. Eleven crore amounts to more than double the population of Myanmar itself.

In September 2017, Union Minister of State for Home Affairs Kiren Rijju had informed Parliament that the Rohingya population in India was 40,000, including 16,000 Rohingyas who were registered with the United Nations (UN) as refugees.

According to the International Migration Report 2017 released by the UN, the number of Bangladeshi migrants residing in India is 3.1 million (thirty-one lakh).

10

ROHINGYA REFUGEES ARE EATING FLESH OF HINDUS

A POPULAR, PREDICTABLE AND oft-used strategy on social media is to foment division along communal lines by spreading misinformation. There are numerous instances, wherein a coordinated and organized attempt to vitiate inter-faith relations has been observed. The tactics employed in this regard are predictable – use of unrelated images and/or videos, or through provocative text. The Rohingya crisis in Myanmar brought attention on Rohingya refugees in India and provided one such opportunity. In the instance that we will talk about here, the nature of the claim accompanying certain photographs revealed the sheer extent to which hatemongers will go in their pursuit of instilling fear, mistrust and hate.

Claim: Rohingyas are 'eating the flesh of Hindus'.

Dainik Bharat published an article in December 2018 titled 'डरावनी खबर – हिन्दू का कतल कर उनका मास खा रहे रोहिंग्या, मेवात का मामला, खबर विचलित कर सकती है' (Horrifying news – Rohingyas are killing Hindus and eating their flesh, a case from Mewat, this news may send shivers down your spine.)

The message seemed to have been shared in the form of a newspaper clipping of an obscure 'news' publication called *Aaj Tak Gurgaon* (not related to the India Today Group).

Fact: The claim made by *Dainik Bharat* is nothing less than diabolical. Using Google's reverse image search, Alt News established that the images have nothing to do with Rohingyas. The photographs are representative of a funeral ritual practised by the Tibetan community, in which a human corpse is placed on a mountain and exposed to scavenging birds. This ritual is popularly called a 'sky burial' and is a traditional funeral custom to bid farewell to the dead.

The images first featured in a blog written in 2009 describing the Tibetan ritual. Alt News traced a National Geographic video as the source of two images.

Reference: https://www.hindustantimes.com/india-news/inside-the-world-of-hindu-right-wing-fake-news-website-dainikbharat-org/story-aPdB03A4LjeIkFBFKmV0vI.html
https://en.wikipedia.org/wiki/Sky_burial

11

ROHINGYA POPULATION GROWTH A MATTER OF CONCERN, YOUNG GIRLS PREGNANT

THE PERSECUTION FACED BY the Rohingya community in Myanmar and their influx into India created a huge political controversy throughout 2017 and 2018. Social media too was not immune to the crisis. Photographs with false and/or misleading narratives were shared by several social media users in order to shape public opinion on the issue.

PHOTOGRAPH OF A YOUNG 'PREGNANT' GIRL

Claim: A photograph of a young girl with an enlarged belly was shared by some social media users. It was claimed that she was from a refugee camp in Rakhine state, Myanmar, was around nine to twelve years old and had been impregnated.

Fact: The claim was false and malicious. Sandy is a twelve-year-old Brazilian girl, suffering from multiple health problems, including a liver condition. The Facebook page of Garrafão do Norte, the place where she lives, had shared her story of strength and perseverance and made an appeal for help. In the video posted on the page, Sandy could be seen talking from her hospital bed. It was her medical condition which had caused an enlarged belly.

PHOTOGRAPH OF A TEENAGER WITH TWO CHILDREN

Claim: A photograph of a young girl holding a baby was shared on social media with the claim that she was a fourteen-year-old Rohingya girl with two children. The posts further claimed that her husband was fifty-six years old, had six wives including this young girl and eighteen children.

9:39 AM - 24 Sep 2017

Fact: The photograph had been taken from a documentary on the Rohingya community by BBC News. The report chronicled the struggle of the community against ethnic persecution. The accompanying narrative – the girl is fourteen years old and a mother of two – was a complete fabrication.

We have noticed that a large percentage of fake news and rumours originate from a small set of websites and social media profiles. These are habitual offenders who quietly delete the original post without any apology after the objective of starting the rumour has been achieved. Beware of news originating from such accounts.

Reference: https://www.nationalheraldindia.com/fact-check/disturbing-hate-campaign-against-rohingyas-gets-exposed-again

12

STATUE OF SWAMI VIVEKANANDA DESECRATED BY MUSLIMS

Claim: In October 2017, a statue of Swami Vivekananda was found desecrated at Bhadohi in Uttar Pradesh. *ShankhNaad,* in a now-deleted tweet, claimed that this was the handiwork of members of the Muslim community, and blamed the media for being 'silent'.

ShankhNaad
@ShankhNaad

(Follow) ⌄

BREAKING: Statue of Swami #Vivekananda "beheaded" / destroyed allegedly by #Muslims in Bhadohi, UP.
Is India Saudi Arabia ? Media silent.

Statue of Swami Vivekananda 'beheaded' allegedly by Muslims in Bhadohi, UP

10:11 PM - 28 Oct 2017

2,776 Retweets **1,368** Likes

Fact: Following these rumours, the superintendent of Bhadohi had issued a clarification stating that one Premchandra Gautam had been arrested. Clearly, an attempt was made to inflame passions between the members of the two communities.

13

JAIN MONK ASSAULTED BY MUSLIMS

Claim: '*Very sad news, yesterday in Karantaka Jain muni attacked by Muslim youths ... No one is safe in Siddaramaiah's Karnataka.*'

This message was tweeted in March 2018 by Mahesh Vikram Hegde, the co-founder of Postcard News, along with a photograph showing a mendicant in an injured condition. Hegde had alleged that this Jain monk had been 'attacked by Muslim youth'.

Fact: Alt News found that the news was first reported by a Jain publication, *Ahinsa Kranti*. Jain muni Mayank Sagar had had a minor accident when he was hurt on his shoulder after being hit by a bike. The incident had occurred in Kanakapura, Karnataka. The editor of the publication, Mukesh Jain, told Alt News about the news posted on his website and denied that the incident had anything to do with members of the Muslim community. Hegde was subsequently arrested for this misinformation and charged under section 153(A) of the India Penal Code (IPC) (promoting enmity between groups).

Reference: https://www.news18.com/news/india/postcard-website-editor-arrested-for-spreading-fake-news-about-muslims-in-karnataka-bjp-leaders-jump-to-his-defence-1703373.html
https://scroll.in/article/873872/arrest-of-postcard-news-co-founder-shines-a-light-on-indias-fake-news-problem
https://www.business-standard.com/article/current-affairs/jain-monk-attacked-my-muslim-youth-man-behind-fake-news-held-in-karnataka-118033000629_1.html

14

MUSLIMS MARCHED ON THE STREETS DEMANDING RELEASE OF RAPE ACCUSED

AN EIGHT-YEAR-OLD WAS RAPED in Mandsaur, Madhya Pradesh, in June 2018. The accused in this case was a Muslim. Since the incident occurred in the backdrop of the filing of the chargesheet in the Kathua rape case of January, an attempt was made to give this incident a communal narrative by suggesting that members of the Muslim community had marched on the streets in his support.

Claim: Members of the Muslim community rallied on the streets of Mandsaur demanding that the perpetrator of the crime be released because the Quran sanctions rape of non-Muslim women. The originator of this rumour was said to be a website called IndiaFlare which published an article titled, 'कुरान में दूसरे धर्म की लड़कियों से बलात्कार जायज़, इरफ़ान खान को रिहा करो' (Rape of non-Muslim girls valid according to Quran, release Irfan Khan). The article carried a photograph which showed Muslim men marching on a street holding placards.

Fact: The photograph posted on top which shows Muslim men marching in support of the accused had been Photoshopped. Alt

News did a Google reverse image search and found that while the march did indeed take place in Mandsaur, it was *in support of the victim and against the accused.* The original photograph is published below the doctored image.

As can be seen, the text on the placard was tampered with. The original text says, '*नहीं सहेंगे बेटी पर वार, बंद करो ये अत्याचार*' *(Won't tolerate attacks on daughters, stop this brutality.)*

Firstpost reported that Muslim groups in the region had strongly condemned the incident and demanded harsh penalty for the accused. Some groups demanded death penalty for the alleged perpetrator and appealed to not allow his body to be buried in any graveyard in Mandsaur or Neemuch.

References: https://www.firstpost.com/india/mandsaur-rape-case-spurs-angry-protests-by-hindu-muslim-organisations-lawyers-refuse-to-represent-accused-4641781.html
https://bangaloremirror.indiatimes.com/bangalore/others/fake-news-buster-mandsaur-march-pics-are-fake/articleshow/64832524.cms

15

'MUSLIMS RESPONSIBLE FOR 95% RAPES IN INDIA IN 2016'

CONCERNS OVER CHANGE IN demographic composition have been used to stir fear. According to a popular 'statistic' circulated on social media in this regard, an overwhelming majority of rapes in India are the handiwork of members of the minority community.

Claim: NCRB report says that India is most dangerous for women. In India, 95 per cent of the rape cases have a Muslim perpetrator. Of the total 84,734 rape cases, 81,000 rapes had a Muslim rapist and 96 per cent of the victims are non-Muslims and with an increase in their population, number of rapes will also increase (translation). Among those who shared this message was Mahesh Vikram Hegde of Postcard News.

Fact: The National Crime Records Bureau (NCRB) does not record crime on the basis of religious denomination. What it tabulates instead is the age group of the victims, and the relation of the offender to the victim.

In an official statement given to Alt News, NCRB had rubbished the rumour, stating, 'It is totally wrong data and complete misrepresentation of facts as NCRB does not collect data on the religion of accused and victims. It is malicious propaganda, which needs to be countered by the law-abiding citizens. Concerned officials have been advised to initiate legal action.'

Reference: https://www.indiatoday.in/fact-check/story/fact-check-claim-linking-muslims-to-96-per-cent-rapes-in-india-falls-flat-1278750-2018-07-06

16

A RATE CARD FOR 'LOVE JIHAD' TO LURE NON-MUSLIM WOMEN

A 'LOVE JIHAD RATE list' was circulated on social media, with a price tag put on non-Muslim women, along with an exhortation to lure them and convert them to Islam. The prices ranged from ₹3 lakh for a Jain girl to ₹6 lakh for a Hindu Brahmin girl to ₹7 lakh for a Sikh girl.

Claim: A rate card is in circulation for luring non-Muslim women.

News channel Times Now used the hashtag #CaliphateConvertsHindus to tweet various aspects of this story. They also tweeted the denominations in the rate-card poster, a screenshot of which can be seen on the next page.

 **TIMES NOW**
@TimesNow

(Follow) ∨

TIMES NOW accesses Conversion rate card
Hindu (Brahmin girl)=5L
Hindu (Kshatriya girl)=4.5L
Hindu (OBC, SC,ST)=2L
#CaliphateConvertsHindus

Retweets   Likes
1,090   556

8:07 AM - 23 Jun 2017

Throwing his hands up in disgust, Times Now editor-in-chief Rahul Shivshankar said on a prime-time show, 'I can't even begin to tell you ladies and gentlemen the kind of insidious fine print that is on this rate card … the caliphate has put a price on your faith.'

Ahmedabad Mirror ran a story in February 2016 titled '*Love Jihad in Vadodara comes with a price tag*' based on this poster. Subsequently, the *Ahmedabad Mirror* story was reported by various other media outlets such as Zee News, One India and *Dainik Bhaskar* (Marathi), India.com and Sahara Samay.

Fact: Alt News found that this particular message had been circulating on social media and WhatsApp for several years, with the earliest version of this provocative message found on a blog titled 'Sikhism and Islam', dating back to February 2010. This blog has exactly one post and the original coloured version of the black-and-white image that *Times Now* showed. There were a number of clues in this message which established that it is fake.

Firstly, the message had the phrase, 'in the name of Allah…… most merciful, most beneficiary', while the usual phrase used is

'In the name of Allah, the most the most merciful'. Such a mistake would be unusual if this had actually been a pamphlet issued by an Islamic organization.

Moreover, the heart-shaped image at the top of the pamphlet gave the most concrete evidence of this poster being a Photoshopped one. The gun-shaped image within the heart is actually the flag of Hezbollah, the Lebanese Shi'a Islam militant group. All this points to the fact that the image has been created for the sake of propaganda using computer software and that there is nothing factual about it.

We found that this particular claim had also made its presence in *Saamna*, the mouthpiece of the Shiv Sena. It had been posted by several pro-Hindutva websites over the years.

References: https://ahmedabadmirror.indiatimes.com/ahmedabad/others/
love-jihad-in-vadodara-comes-with-a-prize-tag/articleshow/50921276.
cmshttps://www.newslaundry.com/2017/06/24/times-now-kerala-isis-
whatsapp-report

17

INDIAN MUSLIMS CELEBRATING PAKISTAN'S CRICKET VICTORY

ANOTHER VIDEO WHICH WAS shared on social media claimed that children and adults were celebrating Pakistan's victory over India. The video showed a hall full of people glued to a screen and cheering loudly. It was claimed that this incident occurred at Mira Road in Mumbai.

Fact: This video is not from India.

A close look at the video reveals the logo of PTV Sports, a Pakistani channel. Alt News also found that the same video had been uploaded on YouTube with the title, 'Pakistani Dawoodi Bohra's Celebration On Pakistan's Win In Champions Trophy against India!'

PTV's broadcast is banned in India and hence this video is either from Pakistan or any other country where PTV is broadcasted. While sports should ideally be watched for the entertainment value and the support of an individual or a group of people for a specific team should not be a reason to deride anyone, India–Pakistan matches are a different cup of tea due to historical reasons.

The basic idea behind circulating these fake videos seems to be to exploit these very emotions linked to an India–Pakistan cricket match and perhaps to propagate the idea that Indian Muslims are anti-Indian/pro-Pakistan.

BUILDING BRAND MODI

PRIME MINISTER NARENDRA MODI is arguably the most popular politician in India at present. On social media, he has a gargantuan following. His image of a 'karmayogi' (a doer) is, in no small measure, due to the constant campaigning observed on social media by networks that openly express support for the BJP. Sympathizers of the party seem omniscient – there are hundreds of pages, groups, handles and accounts which are actively engaged in disseminating the supposed accomplishments of the present regime. This dissemination has regularly taken the form of propaganda.

There are numerous tools – fake quotations, exaggerated claims vis-à-vis economic development, assertions about Modi's work ethic, and so on.

18

QUOTES OF GLOBAL LEADERS SHOWERING PRAISES ON PM NARENDRA MODI

ONE OF THE KEY ingredients that has contributed to Prime Minister Narendra Modi's success is his ability to manage popular perception. The assertion that PM Modi is an administrative genius was sought to be legitimized by his supporters by reiterating that some of the leading public figures in the world in the fields of management, academia and business have endorsed his competence.

Claim: The following statements about PM Modi were reportedly have been made by several leading public figures:

'In my career, I have taught people various marketing theories, but I can't teach marketing skills to Narendra Modi, he knows everything.' – Philip Kotler, marketing guru

'If there's anybody who can teach you better management skills than us, it's the Indian PM; you should listen to his speeches often.' – Louise Richardson, vice-chancellor of Oxford University

'*I am all praise for the Indian PM, the steps he has taken, will bolster the economy and growth rate.*' – Jim Yong Kim, World Bank chairman

'*I have seen many leaders failing to perform under pressure, but Narendra Modi is perhaps the only leader I've come across who's unaffected under pressure.*' – Bill Gates, entrepreneur and philanthropist

The infographics on which these quotes were represented carried the logo of The Fearless Indian, which has a popular presence across social media platforms and regularly posts content in favour of Modi and the BJP.

Fact: Three out of these four statements were denied by those to whom they were attributed. No response was received in the case of the fourth.

Alt News contacted all four individuals who were quoted and got the following responses:

Philip Kotler confirmed that he had made no such statement.

In an email conversation, Louise Richardson's office confirmed that she had not uttered the words ascribed to her in this infographic.

On Jim Yong Kim's alleged statement, World Bank Press Secretary David Theis responded in an email conversation, 'I have looked into the alleged quote from the World Bank, and can find no credible evidence of its veracity. It appears to be extrapolating from something said in 2016.'

Alt News did not receive any response from Bill Gates or his office in connection with the supposed quote. It may be noted that there are no media reports about this quotation.

19

PHOTOGRAPH OF PM MODI AS CENTRE OF ATTENTION OF WORLD LEADERS AT G20 SUMMIT

Claim: Photograph showing that Prime Minister Narendra Modi was the centre of attention at the G20 summit.

'Friends ज़रा इस फ़ोटो को गौर से देखिये, भारत के इतिहास में क्या यह दृश्य देखने को आपकी आंखें तरस गई होंगी' (Friends, look at this photo carefully, it is the scene your eyes were dying to see in Indian history.)

The above text accompanied a photograph which showed Prime Minister Modi seated on a chair, surrounded by heads of government including US President Donald Trump. Looking at the picture, it appears that Modi is the central figure in an important discussion and the others are consulting him and waiting for him to speak.

Another message circulated with the same photograph read, 'आप देख रहे हैं अन्तर्राष्ट्रीय स्तर पे भारत की इज़्ज़त को चार चाँद लगा दिए मोदीजी ने उनको सादर नमनः और जिनको मिर्ची लगी हो वो कृपया इस पोस्ट से दूर रहें।' (You can see how the respect for India has been enhanced on the international stage thanks to Modiji. Best regards to him and those who have been rattled should stay away from this post.)

Fact: It is a Photoshopped image.

In the original image, the seat on which Modi is shown to be seated is empty. The photograph was clicked at the G20 summit held at Hamburg in Germany in July 2017.

There are similar Photoshopped versions of this image showing Russian President Vladimir Putin and North Korean leader Kim Jong Un seated on the (vacant) chair.

This picture is a fake. Screenshot via Twitter

The same image was shared by a Facebook user (the content is no longer available) on 26 April 2018, with the same text. It has been shared more than 54,000 times and 'liked' more than 4,200 times at the time of writing this article.

According to a Business Insider article, the original image was taken by a photographer, Kayhan Ozer, for Getty Images, an American stock photo agency. The authentic image was captioned, 'President of Turkey Recep Tayyip Erdoğan (R) talks with US President Donald Trump (L), accompanied by Foreign Affairs Minister of Turkey Mevlut Cavusoglu (2nd R), during a session within the G20 Leaders' Summit in Hamburg, Germany on July 07, 2017.'

20

NARENDRA MODI BECOMES THE FIRST PASSENGER IN INDIA'S FIRST EVER SEAPLANE

Claim: On Prime Minister Narendra Modi's website (www. narendramodi.in), the headline for one of the stories on 12 December 2017 claimed, 'PM Modi becomes first passenger of India's first ever seaplane!' The article on the website referred to the PM's seaplane ride from Sabarmati river in Ahmedabad to Dharoi dam in Mehsana as part of his campaign ahead of the second phase of polling in the Gujarat elections.

This was, however, shared by the BJP, Sadananda Gowda, Dr Mahesh Sharma, Maneka Gandhi, Times Now, Republic TV, *The*

Economic Times, The Financial Express, India TV and *Business Standard*.

The headline of the article on Narendra Modi's website was later altered.

Fact: The claim is incorrect. The first commercial seaplane service in India was launched way back in 2010.

Alt News fact-checked this claim, searching with the keywords 'seaplane' and 'India', and found that it was far from the truth. Jal Hans, a service which was jointly operated by Pawan Hans, the public-sector helicopter service provider and the administration of the Andaman and Nicobar Islands, was inaugurated in December that year.

Another government initiative to launch a seaplane service in India was by the government of Kerala in June 2013 when the Kerala seaplane service promoted by Kerala Tourism

Infrastructure Ltd was announced to connect the waterways of the state. The project, however, failed to commence owing to protests by the local fishing communities.

Moreover, the attempt to launch seaplane services in India was not limited to the government. Private players had announced seaplane services way back in 2011–12.

India's first seaplane named 'Jal Hans' was first launched in 2010 during my tenure as Civil Aviation Minister which greatly facilitated connectivity & tourism in the Andaman & Nicobar Islands. #seaplane

6:51 PM - 9 Dec 2017

The headline of the article on the PM's website was later altered to state 'PM Modi travels by seaplane'. However, no media house issued a later clarification regarding the same.

21

RETIRED BUREAUCRAT REVEALS THAT PM MODI WORKS 18-20 HOURS A DAY

SEVERAL URBAN LEGENDS SURROUNDING Prime Minister Narendra Modi have been circulated on social media. For instance, the claim 'Narendra Modi had been declared the best prime minister in the world by UNESCO' or Julian Assange of Wikileaks fame stating that 'Modi is incorruptible'.

Similarly, an elaborate hoax started by certain supporters of PM Modi was about how a bureaucrat who had retired in February 2014 decided to rejoin Modi's Prime Minister's Office (PMO) and the story he narrates about Modi's work ethic. Here's the story.

Claim: PM Modi works 18-20 hours a day. Someone called Manish Malhotra, who is an 'Indian MBA' from the UK and has a close relative in the PMO, is the source of the article. This close relative is referred to as Mr A.

Fact: It is a hoax.

Alt News did some basic fact-checking to ascertain the veracity of this story. The Facebook post shown above was of May 2016. Here is what we found.

The post claimed that Mr A has been an officer in the government for the last forty-four years and retired in February 2014. The typical retirement age of IAS/IPS/IFS officers is sixty. Forty-four years of service would mean that he was appointed at the age of sixteen! The minimum age at which a person can join the civil service is twenty-two.

We checked the list of officers listed on the PMO website and googled each one of them for their current employment status. Only three officers in the PMO were among retired IAS/IPS/IFS officers – Nripendra Mishra, Ajit Doval and P.K. Mishra. None of these officers retired in February 2014 or anywhere close to it. Nripendra Mishra's age is around seventy-three and Doval's is seventy-four, so they retired almost a decade ago and much before 'Mr A' supposedly retired. P.K. Mishra's age is sixty-nine, so he retired at least six to eight years ago, again much before February 2014. 'Mr A' is nowhere to be found in the list of officers on the PMO's site.

22

BJP, THALER AND DEMONETIZATION

Claim: 'This is a policy I have long supported. First step towards cashless and good start on reducing corruption.'

These were the words of economist Richard Thaler on demonetization, announced by the central government in November 2016. Soon after Thaler was awarded the Nobel Prize in Economics for 2017, BJP supporters led by Amit Malviya, the BJP IT cell head, went all out to claim through this tweet that Thaler had wholeheartedly supported demonetization.

Fact: Malviya and others had cherry-picked. 'Really? Damn,' was Thaler's reaction when he was told about the new ₹2,000 note in the place of the discontinued ₹500 and ₹1,000 notes. Introduction of the ₹2,000 note negated the objectives of going cashless and reducing corruption, which Thaler supported. This part of Thaler's response was conveniently not disclosed.

Moreover, Thaler later clarified his views on demonetization. The concept was good as a move towards a cashless society to impede corruption but the rollout was deeply flawed and the introduction of the ₹2,000 note made the motivation for the entire exercise puzzling, he had said.

23

FORBES DECLARED MODI GOVERNMENT AS 'MOST TRUSTED IN THE WORLD'

Claim: Narendra Modi's government is the 'most trusted in the world'.

Multiple media organizations had claimed that the Narendra Modi-led government is the 'most trusted in the world'. The basis of this claim was certain data which was published by *Forbes* in 2017. According to *Forbes*, India had topped the list of selected countries which have the most confidence in their governments. Canada, Turkey and Russia came in the second, third and fourth places respectively.

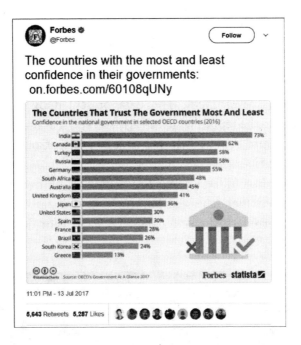

Soon after *Forbes* published this data, several news organizations reported the same news. Some of the news headlines were as under (later edited):

'India tops global index of countries with the most confidence in their government' – *The Times of India*

'With support of 73% Indians, PM Narendra Modi's government most trusted in world: report' – *NDTV*

'Indians top OECD survey on public confidence in the government, Canada comes second' – *Scroll*

Fact: The subheading in the *Forbes* graphic clearly said, 'Confidence in the national government in selected OECD countries (2016)', the operative word being 'selected'. The Organisation for Economic Co-operation and Development (OECD) is an intergovernmental economic organization with thirty-five member countries. Out of the thirty-five countries, *Forbes* had selected fifteen countries and their article was based on data for these.

OECD relies on the 'Confidence in National Government' section from the Gallup World Poll for its section on 'Confidence in National Government'. The data presented by *Forbes* was sourced from the report, which clearly showed that India at 73 per cent ranks third behind Switzerland at 80 per cent and Indonesia at 80 per cent.

Not only had India not topped the list of countries with most confidence in their national government, the statistics for the Indian government showed a massive 9 per cent decline from 2007 to 2016.

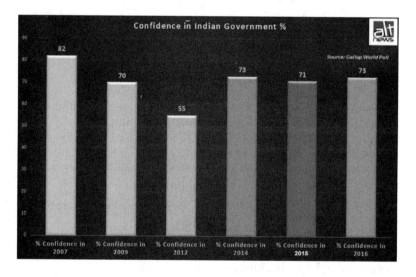

From the data above, it can be seen that India had the lowest ebb in the recent years in 2012 with 55 per cent of the people surveyed having confidence in the national government. The highest point seen in recent years was during the United Progressive Alliance (UPA1) government in 2007 with 82 per cent of the people surveyed having confidence in the national government. This is also in line with UPA2 coming in power in 2009 for the second term. While National Democratic Alliance (NDA) government has been consistent at 73 per cent in 2016, 71 per cent in 2015 and 73 per cent in 2014, it is definitely not the most trusted in the world.

References: India data: https://timesofindia.indiatimes.com/india/india-tops-global-index-of-countries-with-the-most-confidence-in-their-government/articleshow/59588709.cms

https://www.ndtv.com/india-news/indian-government-in-top-3-most-trusted-in-the-world-report-1724682

https://scroll.in/latest/843765/indians-top-oecd-survey-on-public-confidence-in-the-government-canada-second

24

RUPEE FELL BY ONLY ₹1 UNDER THE MODI GOVERNMENT

Claim: Since 2014, the rupee-dollar exchange rate has slipped by only one rupee.

'Under gold medalist Harvard economist 1 Dollar – Rs 39 (2008) 1 Dollar – Rs 68 (2014). Under Chaiwala 1 Dollar – Rs 68 (2014) 1 Dollar – Rs 69 (2018). What this all Ranty-Rona all about? [sic]'.

This message was said to have been shared by @squintneon and several pro-BJP social media users when the government was facing heat over the value of the rupee which had slipped to the then all-time low against the dollar, in June 2018.

With the hashtag #RupeeAllTimeLow, the viral message questioned the public rage against the rupee's lifetime record fall against the dollar by suggesting that the rupee versus dollar equation deteriorated much more during UPA2 than during the present regime, and that the rupee-dollar exchange rate had slipped by only one rupee in the period 2014–2018.

Comrade Squinty
@squintneon

(Follow)   ∨

Under gold medalist Havard economist

1 Dollar - Rs 39(2008)
1 Dollar - Rs 68 (2014)

Under Chaiwala

1 Dollar - Rs 68(2014)
1 Dollar - Rs 69(2018)

What this all Ranty-Rona all about?

11:10 PM - 28 Jun 2018

Fact: The claim is false.

The post suggested that the value of INR against USD when Dr Manmohan Singh demitted office and Narendra Modi assumed office was ₹68. However, the value of the rupee against the US dollar on 17 May 2014, the day Singh demitted the office of prime minister, was ₹58.57. In the period from 1 January 2014 to 16 May 2014, the INR-USD exchange rate was highest on 27 January 2014 at 1 USD = 63.10 INR, whereas the exchange rate of USD to INR on 26 May 2014, the day Narendra Modi was sworn as the prime minister of India, was ₹58.66.

US Dollars (USD) to Indian Rupees (INR) exchange rate for May 26, 2014			
Convert	To	Result	Explain
1 USD	INR	58.6600 INR	1 US Dollar = 58.6600 Indian Rupees on 5/26/2014

Thus, the claim that the value of INR against USD has depreciated by just ₹1 in the period 2014–2018 stands patently false as the value of INR to USD when Modi assumed office was ₹58.66, while the present value is in excess of ₹68.

PORTRAYING OPPOSITION OPPOSITION PARTIES AS ANTI-HINDU

THE AGGRESSIVE PROJECTION OF Prime Minister Narendra Modi and the BJP is concomitant with pervasive attempts to malign the political opposition. The BJP's support system on social media has worked overtime to portray political opponents as either anti-national, anti-Hindu or dictated by selfish personal interests. Another tactic is to spread misinformation about the policy frameworks of states governed by non-BJP parties.

25

KARNATAKA SCHOOL TEACHES QURAN VERSES TO PUPILS

DISINFORMATION TARGETING POLITICAL LEADERS and/ or parties continued well after assembly elections had ended in Karnataka in 2018. A common strategy of the propaganda pages is to use fake news to create a narrative that the Congress is against the interests of Hindus. In July 2018, a video was circulated on social media to show how the Congress-Janata Dal (Secular) (JD[S]) government in Karnataka was 'discriminating' against Hindus and Hinduism through their education policy.

Claim: A video which was said to have gone viral on social media showed a schoolteacher teaching verses of the Quran to her pupils. The narrative claimed that the video was from a school in Karnataka.

Amit Mishra (अमित मिश्र)
@amitkalraj

(Follow) ⌄

In Karnataka the teacher in school is teaching Namaz to Hindu children.
Now this news is ignored by media. If the Gita is taught in any Madarsa.. till now the whole media might have forced the govt to resign.
   know how our religion is being destroyed by these secular parties.

Fact: It turned out that the video in circulation was misleading. It was merely one part of a two-part video. The school in question is the Vidhyadeep Vidhyalaya, a kindergarten in Shivamogga. The second video showed another teacher teaching the students shlokas or verses from the Bhagavad Gita. The exercise was conducted as rehearsal for a programme to be held in the school on Independence Day and included recitation of verses from the Gita, the Quran and the Bible. Despite the inclusiveness of the teaching, only the part referring to the Quran was shared on social media.

26

POLICE BRUTALITY AGAINST SABARIMALA DEVOTEE CAPTURED ON CAMERA

WITH THE RECENT VERDICT of the Supreme Court allowing women of menstruating age entry into the Sabarimala temple in Kerala, massive protests broke out in the state. On social media, a coordinated campaign targeted the state government, projecting it as the 'enemy of the Hindus'.

Claim: Brutal police action on protesting Sabarimala devotee.

'In the eyes of this devotee There is No Fear of brutality There is No fear of oppression This is the Power of Faith #Sabarimala #Ayyappa' [sic].

This message was tweeted by Delhi MLA Kapil Mishra, along with a photograph of a man in the attire of Ayyappa devotees, seen holding an idol. A policeman's foot was visible kicking the man on his chest, suggesting that the Ayyappa devotee in the picture was a victim of police brutality.

Kapil Mishra ☑
@KapilMishra_IND

(Follow) ⌄

In the eyes of this devotee

There is No Fear of brutality
There is No fear of oppression

This is the Power of Faith
#Sabarimala #Ayyappa

5:02 PM - 2 Nov 2018

1,401 Retweets 2,775 Likes

Fact: Image is from a photoshoot.

The photograph was called out on social media by a journalist, Bobins Abraham, who tweeted that a photoshoot of a man named Rajesh Kurup was being circulated as high-handedness by the Kerala police with Ayyappa devotees.

Alt News reached out to Rajesh Kurup, who confirmed to us that the pictures were part of a photoshoot and that the one shared by Kapil Mishra had been shot not too long back.

Kurup, a Rashtriya Swayamsevak Sangh (RSS) worker, was arrested under IPC Sections 153, 500 and Sections 120 and 118 of Kerala Police Act for posting fake pictures of police atrocity. He was later released on bail.

Reference: https://twitter.com/kapilmishra_ind/status/1058321023 244873729?lang=en

https://timesofindia.indiatimes.com/city/kochi/rss-man-held-for-circulating-fake-pics/articleshow/66522443.cms

27

PAKISTANI FLAGS SPOTTED!
A COMPILATION

THE PAKISTANI FLAG IS ubiquitous in India, if one were to go by social media. Alt News has observed that ahead of every election, the national flag of Pakistan is spotted, and that too mostly in rallies held by the Congress party. The rumours have a distinct pattern – the flags are only 'spotted' in non-BJP states and opposition rallies. The clearly aim is to raise doubts about their nationalism. There is also a conscious attempt to somehow link the minority community to Pakistan. Here is a compilation of such instances.

PAKISTANI FLAG WAVED AT CONGRESS RALLY IN KARNATAKA

Claim: Ahead of the assembly elections in Karnataka in May 2018, a video posted on social media showed a green-coloured flag at a political rally. It was claimed that the rally was held by the Congress party, and that the Pakistani flag was waved during it.

Fact: To a layman, any green-coloured flag may pass off as the Pakistani flag, if one overlooks the details. The flag in question was not the Pakistani flag. It was of the Indian Union Muslim League (IUML), a political party based in Kerala. The same video was recirculated after the Congress and the JD(S) formed the government in the state.

ASHOK GEHLOT WAVED PAKISTANI FLAG AT CONGRESS RALLY

Claim: Congress leader and Rajasthan CM Ashok Gehlot had waved the national flag of Pakistan. To bolster this claim, a video was circulated, ahead of the assembly election held in Rajasthan in December 2018.

Mahesh Vikram Hegde
@mvmeet

Follow ⌄

Can you identify the man behind the green
flag?

I feel he was a chief minister of a state under
the Congress party

Look how he waved the green flag

0:10   14.8K views

9:28 AM - 29 Nov 2018

1,350 Retweets 1,661 Likes

Fact: Once again, a religious banner was falsely claimed to be
the flag of Pakistan. That is not all. After the poll verdict was
announced – in which the Congress party emerged as the winner
– social media posts claimed that the Pakistani flag had been
waved at a victory rally held by the party in the state. This too
was false.

PAKISTANI FLAG SPOTTED IN UTTAR PRADESH

'*Uttar Pradesh, Gonda: Pakistani flag hoisted on an electricity pole, created tension*' (translated)

Claim: The above message was allegedly posted by the television news channel News18India in July 2017, along with a video which showed a green-coloured flag atop an electricity pole. The channel reported that the incident had occurred at Gonda.

 **News18 India** ✓
@News18India

Follow ⌄

#UttarPradesh गोंडा: बिजली के पोल पर लहराया पाकिस्तानी झंडा, मचा हड़कंप

⊕ Translate from Hindi

गोंडा: बिजली के पोल पर लहराया पाकिस्तानी झंडा, मचा हड़कंप– **News18 हिंदी**

Fact: Twitter users were quick to point out that the flag seen in the video was not the Pakistani flag but a religious banner. Gonda police clarified that it was not the Pakistani flag but one which had an inscription in Urdu that can be roughly translated as 'there is no one worthy of worship but Allah'.

A similar error in recognizing the Pakistani flag has been made in the past by other news organizations.

PAKISTANI FLAG IN WEST BENGAL

The state of West Bengal has often been in the crosshairs of purveyors of misinformation. The TMC government has been targeted for alleged appeasement of the minority community in the state, at the expense of the majority community. One way in which this accusation finds expression is through social media posts, many of which are inciteful in nature and seek to build a narrative of persecution of the Hindu community.

Claim: A collection of photographs from the streets of Kolkata was circulated on WhatsApp in December 2018. The streets could be seen adorned with green-coloured flags. Expectedly, the claim here was that these are Pakistani national flags. It was alleged that these flags were hoisted in Kolkata in celebration of the newly elected mayor.

Fact: Once again, social media users had confused the generic Islamic banner with the Pakistani flag.

In another instance, a video showed a green-coloured flag hoisted on the rear windshield of a bus that was claimed to be the Pakistani flag, put up on a 'bus full of Muslims from West Bengal'. Here too, the claim was false.

Reference: https://www.timesheadline.com/india/false-news-news-18-india-accused-muslims-hosting-pakistani-flag-6738.html

RAHUL GANDHI – THE FAVOURITE FOR TARGETED PROPAGANDA

POLITICAL LEADERS ARE OFTEN maligned on social media. Use of Photoshopped images is one popular tactic to do so. Among political leaders, Congress President Rahul Gandhi has been a hot favourite. Gandhi is ridiculed in myriad ways on social media. The instances given below are an illustration.

28

RAHUL GANDHI AND POTATO FACTORY

'*AISI MACHINE LAGAUNGA, ISS side se aaloo ghusega, uss side se sona niklega.*' (I will install such a machine that it will convert potato into gold.)

Claim: Rahul Gandhi had become the butt of jokes after a video clip of him saying the above was circulated on social media. Ludicrous as it may seem, it has become a legend of sorts.

Fact: What was shared was merely a curtailed version of a longer video. Rahul Gandhi was referring to the promises made by PM Narendra Modi. Gandhi was speaking at a poll rally in Patan, Gujarat. He had said that this was what PM Modi had promised to potato farmers – placing a machine that will magically change potato to gold. The part where he referred to the prime minister was conveniently left out, in order to make it seem as if these were Rahul Gandhi's words.

Claim: The potato allegory doesn't end there. It was famously claimed that Rahul Gandhi had talked about setting up a 'potato factory' for farmers. The basis of this claim was once again a video clip, in which Gandhi could be heard saying the same.

Fact: This too was an instance of a video clip which was truncated. Listening to the longer, original version of the video made it clear that Rahul Gandhi had referred to the setting up of a factory of potato chips, not potatoes.

29

RAHUL GANDHI SIGNED SOMNATH TEMPLE REGISTER AS A 'NON-HINDU'

CAMPAIGNING WAS ON IN full swing ahead of the assembly elections in Gujarat in December 2017, when the two principal political parties made a last-ditch effort to woo the electorate. Congress President Rahul Gandhi visited the iconic Somnath temple in Gujarat in November 2017, after which controversy erupted on social media over his religious affiliation.

Claim: Rahul Gandhi had signed the temple trust register at the Somnath temple under the section for 'non-Hindus'.

Origin: A tweet by a journalist claimed, 'Congress vice-president Rahul Gandhi visited the Somnath temple. Signed the temple trust register for non-Hindus. Ahmed Patel also registered.'

BJP IT cell head Amit Malviya raised doubts about, 'Gandhis lying about their faith'. Several sources reported the controversy about the 'non-Hindu' entry for Rahul Gandhi. The incident was covered extensively on prime-time TV.

Zee News ran the story with the title '*Rahul ko Hindu hone ka garv nahi*?' with the hashtag #RahulHinduVivad, whereas

Republic TV ran the hastag #RahulHinduorCatholic and asked questions such as 'When you were twenty-seven-years old, the *New York Times* (NYT) listed you as a Catholic. Did you correct them?' and 'Did you, despite accepting the NYT description as a Roman Catholic, call yourself a "Brahmin" in 2012? Different descriptions for different geographies?' Times Now conducted a prime-time debate at 8 p.m. and 9 p.m. with the hashtag #RagaSomnathSelfGoal.

Fact: In a detailed comparison done by Alt News, it was revealed that the handwriting in the register which Gandhi had allegedly signed did not match with the handwriting of the Congress president. Moreover, the entry of Rahul Gandhi and Ahmed Patel's names in the register seemed to have been done by one person. Also, Ahmed Patel's name had been misspelled as Ahemad Patel while Rahul Gandhi's was written as 'Rahul Gandhiji'. It is highly unlikely that Patel would misspell his own name or the Congress president would put down his name as Rahul Gandhiji.

Congress maintained the stance that neither Rahul Gandhi nor Ahmed Patel signed the register. They shared a photo of the visitors' book where Rahul Gandhi had signed. In a follow-up, Firstpost spoke with Somnath temple trust's secretary P.K. Laheri who stated that Rahul Gandhi only signed the visitors' book and nothing else, an assertion which is line with the Congress party's defence.

References: https://twitter.com/amitmalviya/status/9358142065149 74720
https://indianexpress.com/article/opinion/columns/the-most-hindu-of-them-all-religious-identity-of-political-leader-rahul-gandhi-5065765/
https://twitter.com/Zee24Kalak/status/935799510541860864
https://twitter.com/TejashModiLive/status/935867092846256128
https://twitter.com/ZeeNews/status/935838642420908032
https://www.firstpost.com/politics/rahul-gandhi-a-non-hindu-somnath-temple-secretary-tells-firstpost-congress-vp-signed-visitors-book-nothing-else-4233725.html

30

RAHUL GANDHI SPOTTED VIEWING IMAGE OF BIKINI-CLAD WOMAN ON HIS MOBILE PHONE

Claim: Rahul Gandhi was checking out a photo of a scantily clad woman on his mobile phone.

फ़ोटो कभी झूट नहीं बोलती ... देख लो राहुल गाँधी क्या कर रहा है (Photographs never lie ... look at what Rahul Gandhi is doing.)

With these words, a photograph of Rahul Gandhi checking out an image of a bikini-clad woman on his mobile phone was circulated on social media and shared several times.

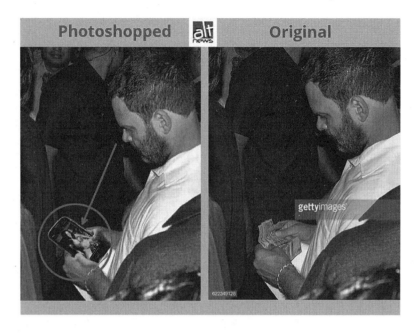

Fact: It is a Photoshopped image.

A simple reverse image search on Google helps reveal the original photograph, in which no mobile phone can be seen in Rahul Gandhi's hand. The photograph was taken in November 2016 when the Congress president had arrived at a bank in New Delhi to exchange his old currency in the aftermath of the announcement of demonetization on 8 November 2016. The original photograph has been posted on the website of Getty Images and shows Rahul Gandhi holding currency notes in his hand.

31

RAHUL GANDHI STUMPED BY A 14-YEAR-OLD IN DUBAI

Claim: Congress President Rahul Gandhi stumped by questions posed by a fourteen-year-old girl: '*Rahul Gandhi dumbfounded in Dubai by little girl's questions*'.

The above was the claim of an article on MyNation, according to which, during Rahul Gandhi's visit to Dubai in January 2019, a fourteen-year-old girl asked him two questions that stumped him. The write-up says that the first question she asked 'was on how Rahul Gandhi, who speaks about how caste distinction is rampant, embraced Hinduism while applying ashes on his forehead in Gujarat and wore the kufis (traditional cap that Muslims wear) while visiting Kashmir', and the second question was, 'Congress prides itself for having ruled India for several decades. The welfare and development that were not achieved then, will be done now? [sic]'

The article adds that the questions embarrassed the Congress president who 'dismissed it with a smile' and the live telecast was cut by the Congress party. The article by MyNation had no accompanying video to back its claim.

Fact: It is a false claim.

Alt News found out that the photograph of the girl which was used in the MyNation article was actually three years old and had been shot at a school in Mumbai.

Moreover, journalists who covered Rahul Gandhi's public events in Dubai confirmed to Alt News that no such interaction had taken place between Gandhi and a fourteen-year-old girl. The lone teenage girl who was present at one of the events featuring Rahul Gandhi confirmed in a Facebook video posted by her father that she had not asked any such question to him and that the news report suggesting the same was not true.

Reference: https://www.mynation.com/news/rahul-gandhi-dumbfounded-dubai-little-girl-questions-pl8fjb

32

PHOTO OF RAHUL GANDHI WITH PORTRAIT OF AURANGZEB IN THE BACKGROUND

AN IMAGE OF RAHUL Gandhi captioned, 'इन देशभक्तों ने यह कौन से देश भक्त की तस्वीर लगा रखी है' (Which nationalist's portrait have these patriots put up?) was shared by pro-Hindutva pages on Facebook. The text sarcastically pointed out a highlighted photo frame with a painting Aurangzeb, asking whether it was a picture of a patriot.

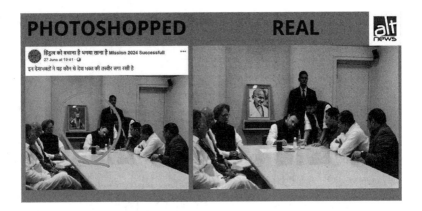

Fact: It is a Photoshopped image.

The original photograph had a portrait of Mahatma Gandhi in the background.

Alt News did a Google reverse image search and found a list of news reports on Rahul Gandhi filing his nomination for Congress president. An article published in *The Indian Express* on 4 December 2017 was titled, 'Congress hails Rahul Gandhi's elevation as beginning "new era": Who said what'. The original image has a Mahatma Gandhi painting in the background.

At a time when social media is rife with Photoshopped images, users can utilize image verification tools like Google reverse image search, which come in handy in debunking misinformation. In this case, however, it is plain ridiculous to believe that a political party would have a picture of Aurangzeb on its wall. Posts like these are aimed at the most gullible who unfortunately tend to believe and share such content.

33

KHALISTANI SUPPORTERS PARTICIPATED IN RAHUL GANDHI'S EVENT IN THE UK

Claim: *'ABSOLUTE SHOCKER!!! At the Indian Overseas Congress meeting in London, anti-India, pro-Khalistani protesters are participating in the event. @RahulGandhi you owe a serious explanation for this dangerous, anti-national narrative being created against India. #RahulGandhiInLondon' [sic].*

The above message, posted by Priti Gandhi, a BJP office-bearer, claimed that separatist elements had participated in an event held in London in which Rahul Gandhi was present.

Priti Gandhi ✔
@MrsGandhi

Following ∨

ABSOLUTE SHOCKER!!!
At the Indian Overseas Congress meeting in
London, anti-India, pro-Khalistani protesters
are participating in the event. @RahulGandhi
you owe a serious explanation for this
dangerous, anti-national narrative being
created against India. #RahulGandhiInLondon

Fact: The claim is false.

The event had been gatecrashed by four Khalistani supporters
who had managed to evade security. This was confirmed by
Naomi Canton, *The Times of India* correspondent in the UK. This
was also admitted by one of the protesters who had gatecrashed
the event, according to a report by *The Times of India*.

Reference: https://twitter.com/mrsgandhi/status/1033679759828348931
https://twitter.com/naomi2009/status/1033987907030269953

PM MODI
AND THE BJP
TARGETED

IN THE EARLY DAYS of social media platforms, the usual trend was the sheer dominance of pro-BJP networks, which were way ahead of networks opposed to the BJP in disseminating misinformation. This dominant presence on social media had manifested itself through a deluge of misinformation which was specifically targeted at political parties and personalities. Of late, however, it has been observed that the others have 'stepped up their game'. Now, political misinformation is no longer exclusively targeted at non-BJP parties. There is a flurry of misinformation 'from the other side', which actively targets the BJP and Prime Minister Narendra Modi, mostly through deployment of the same tactics used by the pro-BJP ecosystem.

34

FOOTBALL JERSEY WITH 'MODI 420' WRITTEN ON IT

Claim: *'इतिहास में इतनी बेइज़्ज़ती किसी प्रधानमंत्री की नहीं हुई! क्या फीफा वालों ने भी पहचान लिया की कौन, क्या है'* (No Prime Minister has been so insulted in history. Has FIFA also understood who he is, what he is).

A photograph of Prime Minister Narendra Modi was shared widely on social media along with this message. In the image, PM Modi can be seen with FIFA President Gianni Infantino who is holding a jersey with the words 'Modi 420 living football FIFA'. PM Modi was on a three-day tour to Argentina to attend the G-20 summit.

Fact: The picture is Photoshopped.

The original text 'G20' which is present in the image was replaced with '420'. The original image was posted on the official Facebook page of Prime Minister Narendra Modi. The post thanked FIFA President Gianni Infantino for the football jersey. It said, 'Impossible to come to Argentina and not think about football. Argentinian players are tremendously popular in India. Today, received this jersey from FIFA President Gianni Infantino. I thank him for the kind gesture.'

35

ALOK VERMA CALLED MODI 'MOST CORRUPT PM IN INDEPENDENT INDIA'

Claim: '*पूर्व सीबीआई निर्देशक अलोक वर्मा ने दिया इस्तीफा, पत्र लिखकर नरेंद्र मोदी को बताया आज़ाद भारत का सबसे भ्रष्ट प्रधानमंत्री*' (Former CBI Director Alok Verma resigns. He wrote a letter calling Narendra Modi the most corrupt prime minister of independent India).

The above message was shared along with a picture of former CBI chief Alok Verma, whose removal had led to controversy. The picture apparently had a logo of Viral In India, which allegedly posts anti-BJP content regularly.

Fact: The claim is false.

Alok Verma had addressed his resignation letter to the secretary of department of personnel and training (DoPT). In the letter, there was no reference to Narendra Modi.

36

PHOTO OF PM MODI SITTING NEXT TO WOMAN INSIDE AIRCRAFT

Claim: A photograph of Prime Minister Narendra Modi was shared in large numbers on social media. It shows the PM seated next to a woman. Former Canadian Prime Minister Stephen Harper too can be seen in this photo. The message that accompanied the photograph says, 'तो देख लो साहब विदेशी दौरा क्यों करते हैं' (*Take a look at why Saheb goes on foreign tours*).

साहब विदेश दौरे पर ?

Fact: It is a Photoshopped image.

Using the reverse image search tool, Alt News found out that the picture is Photoshopped. In the original image, there was another woman sitting next to PM Modi. This woman was Dr Gurdeep Kaur Chawla, who is an interpreter and has been seen on many occasions with several top political leaders.

37

NARENDRA MODI GARLANDED NATHURAM GODSE'S BUST

Claim: A photograph was circulated which showed two images of Prime Minister Narendra Modi. In the photograph on the left, he is seen garlanding a bust of Mahatma Gandhi and in the photo on the right, he is garlanding a bust of what is being claimed to be the bust of the 'killer of Gandhi', in an allusion to Nathuram Godse, who had assassinated Mahatma Gandhi.

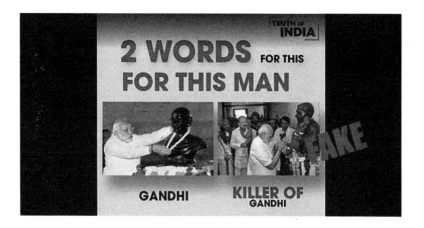

Fact: The claim is false.

In the photograph on the right, PM Modi is garlanding the bust of Deen Dayal Upadhyay, Sangh Parivar ideologue and the founder of the erstwhile Bharatiya Jana Sangh.

Using Google reverse image search, we found an article by the *International Business Times* dated 6 April 2017. The caption accompanying the photograph clearly says that PM Modi was paying tribute to Pandit Deen Dayal Upadhyay.

38

INDIAN ECONOMY PLUMMETED FROM BEING THE THIRD LARGEST TO THE SIXTH LARGEST

IN JULY 2018, ACCORDING to the latest World Bank report, India officially overtook France to become the sixth-largest economy in the world. While this was welcome news, certain sections of social media claimed that the country's economic position had in fact deteriorated, and that it had actually fallen in ranking.

Claim: India had already become the third-largest economy in the world in 2011 (2013 according to some) when UPA-II was in power, and the nation had in fact slipped in the global ranking from third to sixth.

Among those who shared this news were Brijesh Kalappa, spokesperson of the Congress party, and Gaurav Pandhi, former social media head of the Congress party.

Brijesh Kalappa ✔
@brijeshkalappa

(Follow) ⌄

Bhakts are exulting that India has beaten France to become the 6th largest economy in the world. Modi Effect!!
Ahem! India was 3rd Largest Economy in the world in 2011. Manmohan Defect!!

India became third largest economy in 2011: World Bank
In a matter of six years, India emerged as the world's third-largest economy in 2011 from being the tenth largest in 2005, moving ahead of Japan, while the US remai...
thehindu.com

Fact: This is a case of different yardsticks being used for comparison. Articles quoted in the claim refer to Gross domestic product (GDP) according to purchasing power parity (PPP) whereas the news of India surpassing France to become the sixth largest economy in the world was on the basis of nominal GDP.

According to the GDP (PPP) method, India continues to be ranked third. In 2011, India ranked ninth in terms of nominal GDP and third in terms of GDP (PPP).

India was the third-largest economy in the world in 2011 on the basis of PPP and NOT the nominal GDP method, according to which India's rank among the world's largest economies had risen from ninth to sixth. Insofar as GDP (PPP) ranking is concerned, India has maintained its rank as the third-largest economy in 2017.

Methods of GDP calculation: GDP (Nominal)– Nominal GDP is the total value of goods and services produced in a country in a given year at current market prices. It is a quantitative concept which takes into account the total size of economies, focusing on volume of goods and services.

GDP (PPP)– Purchasing power parity is measured in terms of comparing the value of a standard basket of goods across nations. As the term suggests, it is the measure of *purchasing power* of a unit of currency.

Reference: https://twitter.com/brijeshkalappa/status/10172716133420 52352

39

INDIA'S RANKING IN GLOBAL HUNGER INDEX FELL FROM 55 TO 103 IN FOUR YEARS

THE GLOBAL HUNGER INDEX (GHI) 2018 was released in October 2018, positioning India at 103 among 119 nations.

Claim: India's ranking in the GHI has fallen from 55 in 2014 to 103 in 2018.

India's ranking has been much talked about, with several media outlets and members of the opposition criticizing the present government for the 'drop' in the country's ranking.

This was reported by NDTV, *Dainik Bhaskar*, etc. and shared by Rahul Gandhi.

Rahul Gandhi ✓
@RahulGandhi

चौकीदार ने भाषण खूब दिया,
पेट का आसन भूल गये।

योग-भोग सब खूब किया,
जनता का राशन भूल गये।

Translate Tweet

कलंक: देश से भुखमरी दूर करने में पूरी तरह फेल हुई मोदी सरकार, 119 देशों की रैंकिंग में...
विकास के तमाम दावों के बीच सरकार की नींद उड़ा देने वाली एक रिपोर्ट सामने आई है, एक रिपोर्ट
के मुताबिक भारत में भूख एक गंभीर समस्या है और 119 देशों के वैश्विक भूख सूचकांक में भारत...
bhaskar.com

Fact: The claim is misleading.

Alt News studied the GHI reports of the years 2014–2018. At first sight, the reports indicated India's rankings as 55 in 2014, 80 in 2015, 97 in 2016 and 100 in 2017. However, a closer look at the reports prior to 2016 showed a major difference in the way the data was tabulated and presented. Prior to 2016, they included an additional table next to the main table which tabulated all countries which had GHI index of less than 5. Only those which had a GHI index of more than 5 were ranked in the main table.

TABLE 2.1 COUNTRY GLOBAL HUNGER INDEX SCORES BY RANK, 1990 GHI, 1995 GHI, 2000 GHI, 2005 GHI, AND 2014 GHI

Rank	Country	1990	1995	2000	2005	2014
1	Mauritius	8.3	7.6	6.7	6.0	5.0
1	Thailand	21.3	17.3	10.2	6.7	5.0
3	Albania	9.1	6.3	7.9	6.2	5.3
3	Colombia	10.9	8.2	6.8	7.0	5.3
5	China	13.6	10.7	8.5	6.8	5.4
5	Malaysia	9.4	7.0	6.9	5.7	5.4
7	Peru	16.1	12.4	10.6	10.0	5.7
8	Syrian Arab Republic	7.8	6.1	<5	5.1	5.9
9	Honduras	14.6	13.9	11.2	9.0	6.0
9	Suriname	11.3	10.1	10.9	9.0	6.0
11	Gabon	10.0	8.6	7.8	7.4	6.1
12	El Salvador	10.8	8.8	7.9	6.4	6.2
13	Guyana	14.5	10.9	8.1	7.9	6.5
14	Dominican Republic	15.6	11.5	9.9	9.6	7.0
15	Vietnam	31.4	25.4	17.3	13.1	7.5
16	Ghana	27.2	20.2	16.1	11.3	7.8
17	Ecuador	14.9	11.9	12.0	10.3	7.9
18	Paraguay	9.2	7.4	6.8	6.3	8.8
19	Mongolia	20.3	23.1	18.5	14.1	9.6
19	Nicaragua	24.0	19.7	15.4	11.4	9.6
21	Bolivia	18.6	16.8	14.5	13.9	9.9
22	Indonesia	20.5	17.8	16.1	15.2	10.3
23	Moldova	–	7.9	9.0	7.4	10.8
24	Benin	22.5	20.5	18.0	15.3	11.2
25	Mauritania	23.0	18.7	17.1	14.4	11.9
26	Cameroon	23.3	24.6	21.3	16.6	12.6
27	Iraq	8.6	11.9	12.8	11.6	12.7
28	Mali	27.2	27.2	24.8	20.7	13.0
29	Lesotho	13.1	15.4	14.6	15.0	13.1
29	Philippines	20.1	17.5	17.9	14.7	13.1
31	Botswana	15.6	16.5	18.1	16.8	13.4
32	Gambia, The	18.7	20.4	15.5	15.1	13.6
32	Malawi	31.3	28.8	21.9	18.9	13.6
34	Guinea-Bissau	22.6	20.4	20.5	17.3	13.7
35	Togo	23.6	19.4	20.8	18.0	13.9
36	Guinea	22.0	20.9	22.4	18.0	14.3
37	Senegal	18.9	19.6	19.5	14.3	14.4
38	Nigeria	25.9	23.0	17.9	16.7	14.7
39	Sri Lanka	22.2	20.2	17.6	16.8	15.1
40	Guatemala	15.6	16.0	17.3	17.0	15.6
40	Rwanda	30.6	35.1	30.6	24.1	15.6
42	Côte d'Ivoire	16.4	16.6	17.6	16.5	15.7
43	Cambodia	32.9	30.8	28.1	20.8	16.1
44	Nepal	28.4	26.8	25.2	22.2	16.4
44	North Korea	17.9	22.4	22.8	19.3	16.4
44	Tajikistan	–	21.5	22.3	18.8	16.4
47	Kenya	21.5	21.0	20.2	19.5	16.5
47	Swaziland	9.9	12.3	13.5	11.8	16.5
47	Zimbabwe	19.7	22.5	22.0	21.3	16.5
50	Liberia	24.5	28.9	25.1	20.7	16.8
51	Namibia	21.7	22.0	18.4	16.5	16.9
52	Uganda	21.5	22.7	20.2	18.4	17.0
53	Tanzania	23.5	26.8	26.3	20.8	17.3
54	Angola	40.8	38.9	32.3	24.1	17.4
55	India	31.2	26.9	25.5	24.2	17.8

Rank	Country	1990	1995	2000	2005	2014
56	Congo, Republic	22.6	22.7	18.3	18.3	18.1
57	Bangladesh	36.6	34.4	24.0	19.8	19.1
57	Pakistan	26.7	23.3	22.1	21.0	19.1
59	Djibouti	34.1	29.4	28.5	25.6	19.5
60	Burkina Faso	27.0	22.6	26.3	26.5	19.9
61	Lao PDR	34.5	31.4	29.4	25.0	20.1
62	Mozambique	35.2	32.3	28.2	24.8	20.5
63	Niger	36.4	36.1	31.2	26.4	21.1
64	Central African Republic	30.3	30.3	28.1	28.9	21.5
65	Madagascar	25.3	24.9	27.4	25.2	21.9
66	Sierra Leone	31.2	29.0	29.8	29.1	22.5
67	Haiti	33.6	32.9	25.3	27.9	23.0
68	Zambia	24.7	24.0	26.5	24.7	23.2
69	Yemen, Republic	30.1	27.8	27.8	28.0	23.4
70	Ethiopia	–	42.6	37.4	30.8	24.4
71	Chad	39.7	35.4	30.0	29.8	24.9
72	Sudan/South Sudan*	30.7	25.9	26.7	24.1	26.0
73	Comoros	23.0	26.7	34.0	30.0	29.5
74	Timor-Leste	–	–	–	25.7	29.8
75	Eritrea	–	41.2	40.0	38.8	33.8
76	Burundi	32.0	36.9	38.7	39.0	35.6

COUNTRIES WITH 2014 GHI SCORES LESS THAN 5

Country	'90	'95	'00	'05	'14	Country	'90	'95	'00	'05	'14
Algeria	6.6	7.3	5.1	<5	<5	Lebanon	<5	<5	<5	<5	<5
Argentina	<5	<5	<5	<5	<5	Libya	<5	<5	<5	<5	<5
Armenia	–	10.5	9.0	<5	<5	Lithuania	–	<5	<5	<5	<5
Azerbaijan	–	14.8	12.0	5.2	<5	Macedonia, FYR	–	5.6	<5	<5	<5
Belarus	–	<5	<5	<5	<5	Mexico	5.8	5.6	<5	<5	<5
Bosnia-Herzegovina	–	<5	<5	<5	<5	Montenegro	–	–	<5	<5	<5
Brazil	8.8	7.7	6.5	<5	<5	Morocco	7.6	7.1	6.1	6.4	<5
Bulgaria	<5	<5	<5	<5	<5	Panama	11.6	10.7	11.8	9.5	<5
Chile	<5	<5	<5	<5	<5	Romania	<5	<5	<5	<5	<5
Costa Rica	<5	<5	<5	<5	<5	Russian Fed.	–	<5	<5	<5	<5
Croatia	–	5.4	<5	<5	<5	Saudi Arabia	6.6	6.5	<5	<5	<5
Cuba	<5	8.4	<5	<5	<5	Serbia	–	–	–	–	<5
Egypt, Arab Rep.	7.0	6.3	5.3	<5	<5	Slovak Republic	–	<5	<5	<5	<5
Estonia	–	<5	<5	<5	<5	South Africa	7.6	6.4	7.4	7.8	<5
Fiji	6.2	5.3	<5	<5	<5	Trinidad & Tobago	6.7	7.6	6.8	6.7	<5
Iran, Islamic Rep.	8.5	7.3	5.8	<5	<5	Tunisia	<5	<5	<5	<5	<5
Jamaica	6.1	<5	<5	<5	<5	Turkey	<5	5.0	<5	<5	<5
Jordan	<5	5.5	<5	<5	<5	Turkmenistan	–	10.5	9.1	6.9	<5
Kazakhstan	–	<5	7.8	<5	<5	Ukraine	–	<5	<5	<5	<5
Kuwait	15.6	5.3	<5	<5	<5	Uruguay	5.0	<5	<5	<5	<5
Kyrgyz Republic	–	11.2	9.0	5.4	<5	Uzbekistan	–	7.7	8.9	6.9	<5
Latvia	–	<5	<5	<5	<5	Venezuela, RB	7.5	7.3	6.8	5.8	<5

*GHI scores could only be calculated for former Sudan as one entity, because separate undernourishment estimates for 2011-2013 and earlier were not available for South Sudan, which became independent in 2011, and present-day Sudan.

– = Data not available or not presented. Some countries, such as the post-Soviet states prior to 1991, did not exist in their present borders in the given year or reference period.

Note: Countries are ranked according to 2014 GHI scores. Countries with a 2014 GHI score of less than 5 are not included in the ranking, and differences between their scores are minimal. Countries that have identical 2014 scores are given the same ranking (for example, Mauritius and Thailand both rank first). The following countries could not be included because of lack of data: Afghanistan, Bahrain, Bhutan, the Democratic Republic of the Congo, Georgia, Myanmar, Oman, Papua New Guinea, Qatar, and Somalia.

However, since 2016, the reports included the countries with GHI index of less than 5 in the main table and in the ranking, thus causing a shift in the rankings. The image above is part of the 2018 GHI report. The highlighted portion on the top of the table show the 15 countries which have GHI index of less than 5 and these are included in the main table.

TABLE 2.1 **GLOBAL HUNGER INDEX SCORES BY RANK, 2000 GHI, 2005 GHI, 2010 GHI, AND 2018 GHI**

Rank[1]	Country	2000	2005	2010	2018		Rank[1]	Country	2000	2005	2010	2018
	Belarus	5.0	<5	<5	<5		67	Sri Lanka	22.3	21.2	17.9	17.9
	Bosnia & Herzegovina	9.8	7.2	5.1	<5		68	Myanmar	44.4	36.4	25.9	20.1
	Chile	<5	<5	<5	<5		69	Philippines	25.9	21.6	20.6	20.2
	Costa Rica	6.1	5.6	5.0	<5		70	Guatemala	27.5	23.8	22.0	20.8
	Croatia	6.2	<5	<5	<5		71	Cameroon	41.2	33.7	26.1	21.1
	Cuba	5.3	<5	<5	<5		72	Nepal	36.8	31.4	24.5	21.2
	Estonia	6.7	5.4	<5	<5		73	Indonesia	25.5	26.5	24.5	21.9
	Kuwait	<5	<5	<5	<5		74	Iraq	26.5	24.9	24.4	22.1
	Latvia	6.9	5.0	<5	<5		75	Gambia	27.3	26.2	22.3	22.3
	Lithuania	5.0	<5	<5	<5		76	Swaziland	28.9	27.6	26.7	22.5
	Montenegro	—	—	<5	<5		77	Kenya	36.5	33.5	28.0	23.2
	Romania	8.3	6.8	6.1	<5		78	Cambodia	43.6	29.6	27.8	23.7
	Turkey	10.3	7.3	5.3	<5		78	Lesotho	32.5	29.7	26.3	23.7
	Ukraine	13.6	5.0	<5	<5		80	Benin	37.5	33.5	28.1	24.3
	Uruguay	7.7	8.1	5.4	<5		80	Namibia	30.6	28.4	30.9	24.3
16	Bulgaria	8.2	7.8	7.0	5.0		80	Togo	39.1	36.4	27.1	24.3
16	Slovak Republic	7.2	6.8	5.8	5.0		83	Lao PDR	48.0	35.8	30.3	25.3
18	Argentina	6.7	6.2	5.9	5.3		84	Botswana	33.1	31.2	28.4	25.5
19	Kazakhstan	11.3	12.4	8.8	5.5		85	Côte d'Ivoire	33.7	34.7	31.0	25.9
20	Macedonia, FYR	7.7	8.5	7.0	5.9		86	Bangladesh	36.0	30.8	30.3	26.1
21	Russian Federation	10.1	7.7	7.0	6.1		87	Malawi	44.7	37.8	31.4	26.5
22	Mexico	10.8	9.1	7.7	6.5		88	Mauritania	33.5	29.7	24.8	27.3
22	Serbia	—	—	6.7	6.5		89	Burkina Faso	47.4	48.8	36.8	27.7
24	Iran	13.5	9.4	8.1	7.3		90	Mali	44.2	38.7	27.5	27.8
25	Armenia	18.4	12.8	11.3	7.6		91	Rwanda	58.1	44.8	32.9	28.7
25	China	15.8	13.0	10.0	7.6		92	Guinea	43.7	36.8	30.9	28.9
27	Colombia	11.3	10.8	10.0	7.7		93	Ethiopia	55.9	45.9	37.2	29.1
28	Tunisia	10.7	8.6	7.6	7.9		93	Guinea-Bissau	42.4	40.3	31.0	29.1
29	Trinidad & Tobago	11.7	12.2	12.2	8.0		95	Angola	65.6	50.2	39.7	29.5
30	Georgia	14.6	10.5	8.4	8.1		95	Tanzania	42.4	35.8	34.1	29.5
31	Brazil	13.0	7.0	6.6	8.5		97	Papua New Guinea	30.9	28.2	34.3	29.7
31	Paraguay	13.9	12.5	11.4	8.5		98	Djibouti	46.7	44.1	36.5	30.1
31	Saudi Arabia	11.5	13.8	9.7	8.5		99	Congo, Rep.	37.8	37.2	32.2	30.4
34	Jamaica	8.4	8.2	8.5	8.6		99	Niger	52.5	42.6	36.5	30.4
35	Peru	20.9	18.4	12.5	8.8		101	Comoros	38.0	33.6	30.4	30.8
36	Fiji	9.8	9.3	8.6	9.0		102	Mozambique	49.1	42.4	35.8	30.9
37	Panama	19.8	17.7	12.6	9.1		103	India	38.8	38.8	32.2	31.1
38	Kyrgyz Republic	18.8	14.0	12.4	9.3		103	Nigeria	40.9	34.8	29.2	31.1
39	Algeria	15.6	12.9	10.6	9.4		105	Uganda	41.2	34.2	31.3	31.2
40	Azerbaijan	27.4	17.4	12.3	9.5		106	Pakistan	38.3	37.0	36.0	32.6
41	El Salvador	16.3	13.3	12.8	10.1		107	Zimbabwe	38.7	39.7	36.0	32.9
42	Suriname	16.0	12.5	10.5	10.2		108	Liberia	48.4	42.0	35.2	33.3
43	Dominican Republic	18.4	17.2	13.0	10.3		109	North Korea	40.3	32.9	30.9	34.0
44	Morocco	15.7	17.8	10.2	10.4		110	Timor-Leste	—	41.8	42.4	34.2
44	Thailand	18.3	13.3	12.9	10.4		111	Afghanistan	52.3	43.2	35.0	34.3
46	Oman	13.7	14.7	9.8	10.8		112	Sudan	—	—	—	34.8
47	Mauritius	15.9	15.2	14.1	11.0		113	Haiti	42.7	45.2	48.5	35.4
48	Jordan	12.2	8.5	8.3	11.2		114	Sierra Leone	54.4	51.7	40.4	35.7
49	Venezuela	15.2	12.7	8.4	11.4		115	Zambia	52.0	45.8	42.8	37.6
50	Lebanon	9.1	10.3	8.0	11.7		116	Madagascar	43.5	43.4	36.1	38.0
51	Ecuador	20.6	17.6	14.1	11.8		117	Yemen	43.2	41.7	34.5	39.7
52	Uzbekistan	23.7	17.9	15.6	12.1		118	Chad	51.4	52.0	48.9	45.4
53	Albania	21.6	16.9	15.4	12.2		119	Central African Republic	50.5	49.6	41.3	53.7
53	Turkmenistan	22.0	17.4	15.3	12.2							
55	Guyana	17.8	16.9	15.9	12.6							
55	Mongolia	31.7	24.9	15.8	12.6							
57	Malaysia	15.5	13.0	11.9	13.3							
58	Nicaragua	24.7	17.8	16.4	13.6							
59	Honduras	20.6	17.7	14.7	14.4							
60	South Africa	18.1	20.8	16.1	14.5							
61	Egypt	16.4	14.3	16.3	14.8							
62	Ghana	29.0	22.2	18.2	15.2							
63	Gabon	21.1	19.0	16.7	15.4							
64	Viet Nam	28.2	23.8	18.8	16.0							
65	Bolivia	30.3	27.1	21.8	16.7							
66	Senegal	37.3	27.8	24.1	17.2							

(Left-hand group rows Belarus through Uruguay: 2018 GHI scores less than 5, collectively ranked 1–15[2])

— = Data are not available or not presented. Some countries that do not exist in their present borders in the given year or reference period.

Note: Rankings and index scores from this table cannot be accurately compared with rankings and index scores from previous GHI reports (see Chapter 1).

[1] Ranked according to 2018 GHI scores. Countries that have identical 2018 GHI scores are given the same ranking; for example, Bulgaria and the Slovak Republic are both ranked 16th). The following countries could not be included because of lack of data: Bahrain, Bhutan, Burundi, Democratic Republic of Congo, Equatorial Guinea, Eritrea, Libya, Moldova, Qatar, Somalia, South Sudan, the Syrian Arab Republic, and Tajikistan.

[2] The 15 countries with 2018 GHI scores of less than 5 are not assigned individual ranks, but rather are collectively ranked 1-15. Differences between their scores are minimal.

Thus, the correct absolute ranking of a country in the years prior to 2016 would be calculated by adding the rank in the main table and the count of the countries whose GHI is less than 5. According to the above formula, India's GHI rank was 99 (55+44) in 2014 and 93 (80+13) in 2015. This means that India's ranking has moved from 99 to 103 and not not from 55 to 103 during the period. India continues to suffer from hunger levels categorized as 'serious'.

It must be noted here that GHI ranks/scores are based on a plethora of factors and comparison of year-by-year performance does not arrive at an accurate conclusion. Global Hunger Index itself clarifies in its reports that 'rankings cannot be accurately compared with rankings and index scores from previous reports'.

Reference: https://twitter.com/DainikBhaskar/status/105140576592 2119681
https://khabar.ndtv.com/news/india/global-hunger-index-india-got-103rd-rank-in-ghi-2018-worst-ranking-after-2014-1931809
https://twitter.com/RahulGandhi/status/1051759663308521472

40

AMIT SHAH CALLED BANIYA COMMUNITY 'THIEVES'

AHEAD OF EVERY ELECTION, there is a concerted effort to evoke caste and religion. Social media is no stranger to such attempts. Misinformation surrounding issues of caste and religion has been observed time and again. No political party or unit has a monopoly over dissemination of falsehood. The focus is almost exclusively on divisive issues.

Claim: BJP President Amit Shah called the Baniya community thieves.

A purported newspaper clip which went viral on social media claimed that Amit Shah called the Baniya community 'thieves' and accused them of profiteering. It was suggested that Shah made this statement while rallying, ahead of the Rajasthan elections in Bundi. This claim was shared widely on social media sites such as Facebook and Twitter ahead of the Rajasthan assembly elections, and after polling had ended.

Among those who shared it was said to have been former Union Minister Pawan Kumar Bansal.

Fact: The newspaper clip on which this 'news' was printed was Photoshopped.

Searching for the newspaper clip with different keywords did not bring up any results. It is improbable that a statement where Amit Shah calls members of the Baniya and business community 'cheaters' and 'thieves' went unreported by mainstream media.

Moreover, Alt News looked at news reports and the video of Shah rallying in Bundi. We found out that the BJP chief had given a speech in Bundi on 3 December. However, he did not utter the statements as claimed in the viral newspaper clip.

41

FORMER CHIEF ELECTION COMMISSIONER CREDITED BJP WIN TO EVM HACKING

ELECTRONIC VOTING MACHINES (EVM) usually emerge as the villain after election results are announced by the Election Commission. An unpalatable poll verdict results in rumour-mongering on social media about the susceptibility of EVMs. Integrity is sought to be added to such claims through false attribution to credible sources.

Claim: Quotation attributed to former CEC T.S. Krishnamurthy on the use of EVMs in elections:

'गुजरात और हिमाचल प्रदेश का चुनाव बीजेपी ने ईवीएम हेकिंग से जीता है।' (BJP won the Gujarat and Himachal Pradesh Assembly election by hacking EVMs.) This is what former Chief Election Commissioner T.S. Krishnamurthy was reported to have said.

The quote was allegedly published online as the title of an article, which went on to say *'पूर्व मुख्य चुनाव आयुक्त टीएस कृष्णमूर्ति ने यह कह कर सनसनी फैला दी है कि उत्तर प्रदेश, उत्तराखंड, गुजरात और हिमाचल प्रदेश का चुनाव सिर्फ और सिर्फ बीजेपी ने ईवीएम हेकिंग*

की वजह से जीता है। (Former CEC T.S. Krishnamurthy kicked up a storm by saying that the BJP has won the UP, Uttarakhand, Gujarat and Himachal Pradesh election only on the basis of EVM hacking). The report was published on 21 December 2017, three days after the results of the Gujarat and Himachal Pradesh assembly election were declared.

Fact: It is a fake quote.

In a conversation with Alt News, Krishnamurthy confirmed that he had made no such statement. 'This information is totally wrong, I have never ever expressed any opinion about the working of the EVMs in Gujarat elections. I have only defended the credibility of the Electronic Voting Machines. I have no doubts about its integrity', he clarified.

The report was all the more mischievous as, on 18 December 2017, the day the assembly election results for Gujarat and Himachal Pradesh were announced, Krishnamurthy had in fact issued a statement to the contrary, saying that EVM-bashing must stop as they had 'done their job well'.

42

PHOTOGRAPH SHOWING SIMILARITY OF MANNERISM BETWEEN NARENDRA MODI AND ADOLF HITLER

PRIME MINISTER NARENDRA MODI has often been compared by his detractors with Nazi leader Adolf Hitler. The attempt is to portray PM Modi as dictatorial and fascist, and efforts in this direction have manifested in the form of Photoshopped images of the prime minister.

Claim: Uncanny similarity between Narendra Modi and Adolf Hitler.

Captioned 'spot the difference', an image of Nazi leader Adolf Hitler posing with a child was placed next to an image of Prime Minister Modi, also with a child, and posted on social media. It was also posted by Indian Police Service (IPS) officer Sanjiv Bhatt.

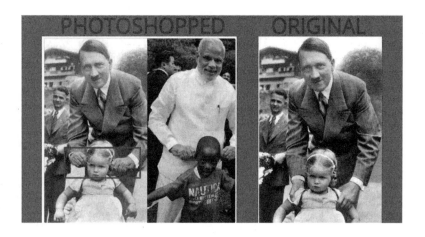

Fact: The picture of Adolf Hitler has been Photoshopped.

A reverse image search on Google reveals that the Hitler image used in the post is Photoshopped. In the original image, he is not holding the child's ears but resting his hands on her shoulders. An article in *The Sun* had published the original image, which was apparently clicked to portray the Nazi leader as a 'personal friend' and guardian of the German youth. Moreover, if one looks closely, PM Modi's left hand has been Photoshopped as Hitler's right and his right hand as Hitler's left.

OTHER TARGETED
POLITICIANS

43

YOGI ADITYANATH QUOTED AS SAYING 'OUR JOB IS TO PROTECT COWS, NOT GIRLS'

THE UTTAR PRADESH GOVERNMENT headed by Yogi Adityanath has been roundly and soundly criticized over its governance priorities. From launching an ambulance service for cows to proposals for introducing a 'cess' for cows, their policies have been hotly debated by netizens on social media.

Claim: Quote on protecting cows instead of women attributed to Uttar Pradesh CM Yogi Adityanath on the basis of a newspaper clip.

'हमारा काम गाय बचाना है, लड़की नहीं।' (Our job is to save the cow and not a girl.)'

The above quote was shared by Avinash Das, a journalist-turned-film director, on social media.

Avinash Das ✔
@avinashonly

Follow

बोलो, इस आदमी को जूते पड़ने चाहिए या नहीं?

🌐 Translate Tweet

8:13 PM - 24 Dec 2018

Fact: It is a fake quote.

Alt News found that the claim originated from a now-deleted satirical website, Rhumor Times.

The statement attributed to Yogi Adityanath first appeared in an article published by the website on 10 April 2018. The 'About Us' section of the website explicitly mentions, 'Rhumor Times is a satire and humour website. The website publishes rumour with humour.'

Reference: https://twitter.com/avinashonly/status/10772132993709 13792

44

SHIVRAJ SINGH CHOUHAN SPOTTED EATING MEAT

POLITICAL CAMPAIGNING WAS ON in full swing before of the Madhya Pradesh assembly elections held in December 2018. Ahead of the polls, social media witnessed a concerted and coordinated effort to sway public opinion, often through misinformation/disinformation.

Claim: Madhya Pradesh CM Shivraj Singh Chouhan spotted eating meat.

'शर्म करो शिवराज चौहान, मीट–मुर्ग़ा खाते हो और जनता के सामने कट्टर हिन्दू होने का दिखावा करते हो. शिवराज की फ़ोटो लीक l' (Have some shame, Shivraj Chouhan, you eat meat while pretending to be a hardcore Hindu in front of the public. Leaked photo of Shivraj.)

The above message was shared by several individuals along with a photograph which showed the former Madhya Pradesh CM eating from a plate containing meat. The image was circulated widely on Facebook and WhatsApp.

Fact: It is a Photoshopped image.

Alt News used Google reverse image search to find the original picture, and found it in an article published by *The Tribune*.

As can be seen in the above original image on the right, Chouhan was not eating meat. The picture was Photoshopped to claim that he is a hypocrite as he professes to be a 'hardcore Hindu', yet he relishes meat.

45

ARVIND KEJRIWAL QUOTED SAYING THAT INDIA SHOULD GIVE UP KASHMIR

DELHI CHIEF MINISTER AND Aam Aadmi Party (AAP) supremo Arvind Kejriwal has been targeted incessantly via misinformation. This tendency was exacerbated after the thumping victory of AAP in the 2015 Delhi assembly elections.

Claim: 'India should concede its right on Kashmir as Kashmiris want independence.'

This quote was ascribed to Arvind Kejriwal and shared in the form of a newspaper clip. This is said to have been in circulation since 2014.

कश्मीर पर भारत अपना हक छोड दे, कश्मीरी लोग आजादी चाहते है : केजरीवाल

पाकिस्तान में जलाए गए भारतीय ध्वज

Fact: The newspaper clip is Photoshopped. It is a fake quote.

There are certain obvious clues that call the bluff of the fake e-paper clip. First, it does not include a date and second, it has some serious grammatical flaws. In the first paragraph, the article addresses CM Kejriwal as '*केजरी* (Kejri)' which is uncharacteristic of a mainstream newspaper. In the subsequent paragraph, a statement by Pakistani PM Nawaz Sharif is not written in the form of a direct quote. As one reads further, similar errors can be identified.

Alt News found the possible origin of the fake clip. In 2014, a similar newspaper clip was posted by a right-wing social media

user, albeit with a changed title and with former Pakistan PM
Nawaz Sharif's photograph in place of Kejriwal's.

कश्मीर पर भारत अपना हक छोड दे, शरीफ ने कश्मीर पर बातचीत
कश्मीरी लोग आजादी चाहते है : केजरीवाल के लिए केजरी को न्योता दिया

46

HAMID ANSARI DISRESPECTED THE NATIONAL FLAG

FORMER VICE PRESIDENT M. Hamid Ansari was repeatedly targeted on social media while he was in office. On more than once occasion, his religion was alluded to and aspersions were cast over his patriotism and commitment. The BJP's national spokesperson Sambit Patra was among those who had posted or shared misinformation with regard to Hamid Ansari.

Claim: Hamid Ansari disrespected the national flag and did not attend Yoga Day.

A photograph of the Republic Day celebration of 2015 was shared widely on social media. The photograph showed US President Barack Obama, Prime Minister Narendra Modi, Defence Minister Manohar Parrikar and Vice President Hamid Ansari. PM Modi and Parrikar could be seen saluting, while the vice president was not. This particular photo was used to demonstrate how Ansari 'doesn't respect his nation'.

#HamidAnsari A Man who doesn't respect his nation while this nation gave him the highest honour of being a VP worst VP we ever had...

Hamid Ansari, the VP who'll be always remembered for his "only Muslim" commentary & not saluting the national flag under excuse of protocol-

Patra, through his tweet, also attacked Ansari over the latter's absence from Yoga Day events. Others who lashed out at Ansari over his absence on Yoga Day included Ram Madhav and Amit Malviya.

Fact: Hamid Ansari followed the Indian Flag Code. With regard to the Yoga Day event, he was not invited.

Patra and others were oblivious to the protocol specified by the Flag Code, which categorically states that the vice president is not supposed to salute if the president is present as the principal dignitary. Since the president is the first citizen of the country, he is considered the principal dignitary at any function he attends. This was the reason why Hamid Ansari was seen not saluting.

Reference: https://twitter.com/sambitswaraj/status/896594718087184 384

47

PRANAB MUKHERJEE PHOTOGRAPHED WEARING AN RSS CAP

FORMER PRESIDENT PRANAB MUKHERJEE'S decision to address RSS cadres at an event in Nagpur was met with a combination of excitement and consternation. While there was a section of citizens who saw this move as a compromise of his ideology, others were more forthcoming, arguing that exchange of contrasting opinions is a vital aspect of democracy. Shortly after Mukherjee addressed the event at the RSS headquarters on 7 June, a photograph began circulating on social media.

Claim: Photograph of Pranab Mukherjee wearing the RSS cap and doing the traditional RSS salute.

Mihir Jha 🖋
@MihirkJha

Follow ∨

What a Brilliant Pic taken by friend
@DarrKeAage, who is attending this
#RSSTritiyaVarsh event as guest....

7:07 AM - 7 Jun 2018

Fact: The image is Photoshopped.

As can be seen in the two images posted on page 126, the picture on the top is the actual one, whereas the one at the bottom has been Photoshopped. The trademark RSS cap, which is part of the organization's official attire, has been added to Mukherjee's head and a hand has been added to the frame to show him doing the traditional RSS salute.

Alt News was alerted by a social media user about the possible source of the photograph.

According to this user, it was first tweeted by one Mihir Jha.

Alt News checked the Twitter account of Mihir Jha, and found that his profile has restricted access. In his 'Bio' section Jha mentions 'Proud to be followed by PM @narendramodi'. Using the exact text provided in the screenshot sent to us, we found the link to the tweet. On clicking the link, we found that the tweet had been deleted. We accessed the cached version of the deleted tweet and managed to obtain a screenshot of the same.

Interestingly, only twenty-three minutes before this image was tweeted, i.e. at 7.14 p.m. IST, Jha had tagged another user @atheistkrishna in a tweet in which he had posted the original photograph. Jha had tweeted to @Atheist_Krishna, 'Can u put one black cap on his head and change hand gestures? Asking for a friend from Congress IT Cell'.

The photograph was shared by none other than Sharmistha Mukherjee, the daughter of Pranab Mukherjee, who claimed that this was the handiwork of the 'dirty tricks department of RSS/ BJP'. It was also shared by Ruchi Sharma, a Congress leader from Haryana, who blamed the BJP IT cell.

The photo was also inadvertently published by NDTV, which later deleted it and issued an apology.

References: https://twitter.com/richard49step/status/1004919820805079040
https://twitter.com/Sharmistha_GK/status/1004778490414051328

48

SONIA GANDHI IS THE FOURTH RICHEST WOMAN IN THE WORLD

Claim: Sonia Gandhi is the fourth richest woman in the world.

A screenshot of a news article was shared on social media, according to which former Congress President and UPA Chairperson Sonia Gandhi is the 'fourth richest politician in the world'.

The claim was alternatively shared as 'fourth richest person in the world' and 'fourth richest woman in the world'.

The screenshot was of an article by *Dainik Jagran* on 4 March 2012. The article was titled, 'The world's fourth richest politician Sonia Gandhi'.

According to the report, American website Business Insider made this claim. As per the site, Sonia Gandhi has a net worth of between US$ 2–19 billion. The same was also believed to have been reported by several other media outlets, including *Aaj Tak*, *One India*, *Dainik Bhaskar* and *Swarajya News*.

Fact: This is a false claim based on an erroneous report.

Alt News looked for the Business Insider story mentioned in all these reports and discovered a 2 March 2012 report titled, 'Meet the 23 Richest Politicians in the World'. Gandhi was fourth on the list, with the article claiming that her net worth was between $ 2–19 billion. The Business Insider story hyperlinked a website named 'World's Luxury Guide as its source.

When Alt News attempted to access the URL provided by *Business Insider*, we were redirected to a 'Not Found' page. Accessing the website's archived pages revealed to us that it had been taken down over a year ago. While Business Insider had provided 'World's Luxury Guide' as the source, World's Luxury Guide had, in turn, provided opensecret.org, forbes.com, bloomberg.com, wikipedia.org and guardian.co.uk as its sources.

Michael McCaul	USA	Member, House of Representatives	$258-380 million
Jane Harman	USA	Member, House of Representatives	$160-326 million
John Kerry	USA	Senator	$181-281 million

Sources: OpenSecrets.org, Forbes.com, Bloomberg.com, Wikipedia.org, Guardian.co.uk; Current as of March 2012

BUSINESS INSIDER · TECH | FINANCE · POLITICS | STRATEGY | LIFE | ALL

Gandhi, the assassinated former prime minister. As leader of the Congress party, Gandhi played a key role in reviving the party's fortune and power.

There's some dispute about her actual net worth, while Forbes doesn't list it. And India's National Election Watch has it listed at about $200,000.

Source: *World's Luxury Guide (based on OpenSecrets.org, Forbes.com, Bloomberg.com, Wikipedia.org, Guardian.co.uk)*

Forbes had published an article in 2011 titled 'India's 100 Richest', which does not include Sonia Gandhi's name. In 2012,

The Guardian had published a report on the world's richest leaders; however, it too did not include Gandhi. On Bloomberg, Alt News back-searched till 2010 but found nothing of relevance. The remaining attribution provided by Business Insider – OpenSecret – has never written any report on the former Congress president.

It was thus evident that there was no basis behind the claims made by Business Insider (and World's Luxury Guide). On 29 November 2013, *Huffington Post* had also published a report on the richest politicians in the world, placing Sonia Gandhi in the twelfth position. However, the former Congress president's name was subsequently removed from the story as the information source, clarified later by the media outlet, was 'called into question'. Here, too, the source was the one stated above. According to the assets declared by her in 2014, Sonia Gandhi's net worth stood at ₹9.28 crore.

The rumours on social media were based on a six-year-old misreport. There is no evidence to suggest that Sonia Gandhi's wealth is to the tune of $2–19 billion as claimed.

Reference: https://www.jagran.com/news/national-sonia-worlds-fourth-richest-politician-9008314.html

https://www.businessinsider.com/richest-politicians-in-the-world-2012-2?IR=T

https://twitter.com/narendramodi_in/status/994229155523940353

49

PHOTOGRAPH OF MANMOHAN SINGH TOUCHING SONIA GANDHI'S FEET

FORMER PRIME MINISTER DR Manmohan Singh has often been portrayed by his detractors as servile to the Nehru-Gandhi family. In this context, a photograph of a turbaned man with Sonia Gandhi was shared widely on social media to show how this presumed servility was not mere perception.

Claim: Dr Manmohan Singh was photographed touching the feet of Sonia Gandhi.

The photo was shared with the caption, 'India's great economist, Dr Manmohan Singh'.

Fact: The person in the photo is not Dr Manmohan Singh.

The photograph in question has circulated across social media channels in recent years, either as an image of the former PM or of Congress MLA Navjot Singh Sidhu touching Sonia Gandhi's feet.

A simple Google reverse image search revealed that the photograph is from 2011 and the man touching Gandhi's feet is a

Congress representative. Getty Images posted the photograph with the caption – 'A representative touches the feet of Sonia Gandhi as Congress General Secretary Rahul Gandhi looks on during the Indian Youth Congress' national level convention of Elected Office Bearers in New Delhi on Tuesday – November 29, 2011.'

Getty Images is an American stock photo agency that supplies licenced images to businesses, creative professionals and the media. Owing to its credibility, most media outlets across the world are subscribed to its database.

Old images are often recirculated with false narratives for political propaganda. Former PM Manmohan Singh has often been in the crosshairs of rumour-mongers who have sought his continuous portrayal as Sonia Gandhi's lackey.

50

PHOTOGRAPHS OF A YOUNG SONIA GANDHI IN A SWIMSUIT

FORMER CONGRESS PRESIDENT AND UPA chairperson Sonia Gandhi has been constantly maligned on social media by her detractors, who seek to cast aspersions over her 'character' by sharing content which 'shows her in poor light'.

Claim: Photographs of a woman in beachwear supposed to be Sonia Gandhi.

'यह लो कांग्रेसी चमचों इसको पहचानों, तुम्हारी राजमाता एंटोनिया सोनिया गांधी है। अब क्या कहोगे चमचों अब भी झूठ लाओगे इसको क्या?' (Look at this, Congressi supporters, and recognize your leader Antonia Sonia Gandhi. Now what what do you have to say? Will you all still claim that this a lie?)

The above message was reportedly circulated along with the photographs on page 134 and were shared by some Facebook pages.

Fact: The photos are not of Sonia Gandhi.

To establish the origin of the photographs, Alt News did a reverse image search the post via Google and found of out that the photographs are actually of Swiss actress Ursula Andress on the sets of the first Bond movie *Dr. No* (1962). The man pictured with Andress is Scottish actor Sean Connery, the first actor to portray the fictional character of British spy James Bond.

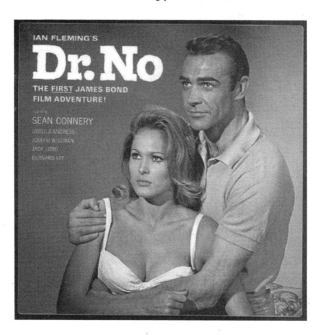

This was not the only time that Sonia Gandhi was targeted through the use of photographs of Western actors. In an earlier instance, a young Reese Witherspoon was passed off as a young Sonia Gandhi.

प्रभात तिवारी,रीवा, मध्य प्रदेश, भारतवर्ष
@PrabhatTw

Follow

@mparunyadav.... Here is Sonia Gandhi as
bar waitress... Pic says all. @TajinderBagga
@malviyamit @RaghuwanshiBabu

10:58 PM - 5 Mar 2016 from Bengaluru, India

FALSE HISTORICAL
CLAIMS

SOCIAL MEDIA, WITH ITS ease of accessibility and use, has become a fertile ground for preposterous historical claims. History is convenient for purveyors of misinformation. It provides legitimacy to present narratives and is thus prone to manipulation. The use of infographics has emerged as a favourite tool. It takes little effort to place a photograph of a historical figure along with a line of text, which is then shared across multiple platforms. Alternately, unrelated photographs may be juxtaposed in order to depict events in a misleading fashion. On some occasions, passages from historical accounts are engineered.

51

MEDIEVAL PAINTING SHOWS KRISHNA POINTING AT THE EID MOON

Claim: Painting of Krishna pointing at the Eid moon.

'Lord Krishna sighting the Eid moon and pointing it [out] to a group of Muslim men and women.'

A familiar painting resurfaced on social media in June 2018 during the time of Eid-ul-fitr, and was also shared by political personalities such as Shashi Tharoor and Yogendra Yadav.

While some users on social media claimed the painting to be the work of Muslim artists, others claimed that it was a reproduction of an 18th-century Rajasthani miniature. However, there was no reference to a source in any of these claims. It is possible that the painting was first posted by *Swarajya* in a 2015 article written by Dipankar Deb.

Fact: Krishna is not pointing at the moon in the painting.

To establish the origin of the painting, Alt News did a reverse image search of the painting via Google and stumbled upon another miniature (housed by The National Museum, Delhi) which depicted similar characters. Its provenance dated back to 18th-century *Pahari* paintings. The Pahari Gharana originated and flourished during the 17th–19th centuries. It developed in Kangra, in north India (named after the then princely state in Himachal Pradesh), becoming the most prominent style of painting.

Alt News reached out to Indian art historian and critic Dr B.N. Goswamy for his insights on the origin of the painting and what it truly depicts.

Arguing against the claims on social media, Dr Goswamy said, 'The present "reading" of it [the painting] is completely meaningless, based as it is, chiefly I think, on the appearance of Nanda, who is dressed like a Mughal courtier: with that kind of beard, and wearing a long jama [clothes] and a sloping turban. There's an anachronic impossibility for a Muslim figure to be seen in the Bhagavata Purana. This is the way Nanda appears in every single folio of this series whenever we see him. Even in this regard, if one notices from close, the jama Nanda wears is clearly a Hindu style jama, tied as it is, in Hindu-fashion, under the left armpit. There is not the slightest doubt about this.'

Alt News's research and the assessment by experts in the field confirms that first, the painting isn't an 18th-century Rajasthani miniature but a Pahari work of art; second, Krishna was not pointing to the Eid moon as shared by many on Twitter; and third, the painting does not depict him as in the company of Muslim men and women.

52

PM MODI: NO LEADER OF THE CONGRESS PARTY MET BHAGAT SINGH IN PRISON

PRIME MINISTER NARENDRA MODI has often targeted the Congress party for having supposedly ignored several stalwarts of the independence movement in their quest to 'glorify one family' over the rest.

Claim: No leader of the Congress party met Bhagat Singh after the latter was imprisoned by the British.

He tweeted, 'When Shaheed Bhagat Singh, Batukeshwar Dutt, Veer Savarkar, greats like them were jailed fighting for the country's independence, did any Congress leader went to meet them? But the Congress leaders go and meet the corrupt who have been jailed.'

narendramodi_in ✓
@narendramodi_in   (Follow) ⌄

When Shaheed Bhagat Singh, Batukeshwar Dutt, Veer Savarkar, greats like them were jailed fighting for the country's independence, did any Congress leader went to meet them? But the Congress leaders go and meet the corrupt who have been jailed: PM @narendramodi

8:24 PM - 9 May 2018

Fact: The claim is not true. Several Congress leaders met Bhagat Singh when he was incarcerated at Lahore jail in 1929.

India's first Prime Minister Jawaharlal Nehru, in his autobiography, *Toward Freedom: The Autobiography of Jawaharlal Nehru*, recalls his meeting with Bhagat Singh when the latter was imprisoned in Lahore jail in 1929. It may be recalled that Bhagat Singh and Batukeshwar Dutt were arrested after they exploded bombs inside the Central Legislative Assembly in Delhi in April 1929. Moreover, Nehru's meeting with Bhagat Singh in Lahore jail was reported by *The Tribune* in August 1929.

The Tribune, Saturday, August 10, 1929.

THE GREAT SACRIFICE MAY BEAR FRUIT

Pt. Jawaharlal's Impressions of Prisoners.

JATINDRA DAS LOOKS FOR RELEASE IN DEATH.

Lahore, Aug. 9.

Pandit Jawaharlal Nehru, in the course of a statement to the press, says :—I visited the Central Jail and the Borstal Jail yesterday and saw Sardar Bhagat Singh, Mr. Batukeshwar Dutt, Mr. Jatindranath Das and all the other accused in the Lahore conspiracy case, who are on hunger-strike. Attempts have been made for many days past to feed forcibly all these hunger-strikers. In the case of some of them the results of this forcible method were so injurious that all forcible feeding had to be given up in the face of a greater danger.

Some of the accused are just maintaining a measure of strength on account of forcible feeding which is given twice a day. Others are in a bad way. Those who cannot be forcibly fed, lest they should die under the force used, cannot obviously survive long now if present conditions continue. They are dying slowly from day to day and the final act in the tragedy cannot be long delayed.

The condition of Mr. Jatindranath Das is specially critical, He is very weak and cannot easily move. He speaks in whisper. He is in considerable pain and looks for release in death. Others whose condition is serious are L. Shiv Varma, Mr. Ajoy Kumar Ghosh and L. Jaidev.

It was very painful for me to meet these extraordinary brave youngmen and to see their manifest suffering. I gathered from them that they would adhere to their resolve, whatever the consequences to their individual selves might be. Indeed they did not care very much for their own selves. They could not undergo such tremendous suffering for a little personal comfort in furture. They feel strongly, however, that the lot of political prisoners in India is bad and must be improved.

The position, as explaind to me by Sardar Bhagat Singh, was that all political prisoners with one exception, if necessary, should be given special treatment. This exception was the case of an actual propetrator of murder.

I can only hope that the great sacrifice which these youngmen are making will bear fruit.—*Free Press.*

References: https://twitter.com/narendramodi_in/status/9942291555 23940353
https://www.indiatoday.in/fact-check/story/fact-check-was-modi-right-about-congress-leaders-not-meeting-bhagat-singh-in-jail-1231140-2018-05-10

53

RAHUL GANDHI: COCA-COLA COMPANY WAS STARTED BY A LEMONADE SELLER

Claim: The person who started the Coca-Cola company used to be a lemonade seller.

This claim was made by Rahul Gandhi who said, 'Is there anyone here who has not heard the name of Coca-Cola company? Has everyone heard of it? Please tell me who started Coca-Cola? Does anyone know? I will tell you who he was. The person who started the Coca-Cola company was a lemonade seller. He used to sell lemonade in America, he used to mix sugar in water. His experience and talent was recognized. He was funded and the Coca-Cola company came into existence.' (translated from Hindi)

The Congress president said this at the party's national Other Backward Class (OBC) convention in Delhi. Attacking the Modi government for failing to provide opportunities to skilled members of the OBC community, Gandhi referred to the Coca-Cola company whose founder, he claimed, used to be a shikanji seller in the USA. 'Shikanji' is similar to lemonade and is typically enjoyed during summer in north India.

Fact: The founder of Coca-Cola company was a pharmacist.
John S. Pemberton was a pharmacist from Georgia, Atlanta.
According to an article by *Time* magazine, Pemberton formulated
a brew – Pemberton's French Wine Coca that included kola nut
and coca-leaf wine – for relief after he suffered a saber wound
during the Battle of Colombus and became addicted to morphine
to mitigate pain. After an alcohol prohibition law was introduced
in Atlanta in 1886, he reformulated the brew without alcohol and
named it *Coca-Cola*. Pemberton, who is described as a 'failed
pharmacist' later began to sell his formula in Georgia's pharmacies.

Reference: https://www.ndtv.com/india-news/rahul-gandhi-says-coca-cola-
maker-sold-shikanji-why-accordingtorahulgandhi-trended-1865748

MALIGNING
JAWAHARLAL
NEHRU

INDIA'S FIRST PRIME MINISTER Jawaharlal Nehru remains a compelling figure of modern Indian politics more than five decades after his death. Revered and vilified in equal measure, few political leaders in the history of the world have attracted admiration and loathing to the degree that Nehru has. The ubiquity of social media has spawned a concerted effort to ridicule and/or demonize him. A common tactic in this regard is the use of fake quotations and statements in order to portray his views and decisions as inimical to national interest. Another tactic is to try and paint him as a philanderer.

54

QUOTE CLAIMING 'I'M MUSLIM BY CULTURE AND HINDU ONLY BY ACCIDENT OF BIRTH' ATTRIBUTED TO JAWAHARLAL NEHRU

Claim: Jawaharlal Nehru had made the following statement: 'I am English by education, Muslim by culture and Hindu merely by accident of birth.'

Social media and the internet has been flooded with the claim of Nehru supposedly having asserted that his identity is primarily shaped by British education and Muslim culture. The quote seeks to paint Nehru as, at the very least, apathetic to Hindus and Hinduism.

Fact: The statement was originally made by a political leader.

A perusal of historical sources tells another story. Alt News used Google Books and found that the quotation appears most prominently in a biography of the Nehrus penned by B.R. Nanda. According to Nanda, these were the words of a Hindu Mahasabha leader. The earliest reference to this statement is found in *A Study of Nehru*, an anthology on Jawaharlal Nehru published in 1959. The volume contained commentaries on India's first prime minister by a number of political leaders from India and abroad.

One of these commentators was N.B. Khare. Khare was a leader of the Hindu Mahasabha, serving as its president in 1950 and 1951. He was a staunch critic of Nehru. His essay in the volume of 1959 was titled 'The Angry Aristocrat'. It is in this essay that this statement first finds mention. Khare claims that Nehru had described himself thus in his autobiography. Interestingly, the autobiography of Jawaharlal Nehru contains no reference to any such statement.

The Angry Aristocrat

EVEN HIS worst critic will have to admit that Nehru is a world
figure in modern times. He is a great man and has been a great
actor on the Indian political stage. But his politics which
resulted ultimately in the acceptance of the partition of
India on a religious basis has caused eternal damage; this is,
indeed, tragic because India's greatness must remain greater
than Nehru's. He has been singularly lucky in being born
the son of Motilal Nehru, a prince among lawyers, and later
in having become the heir of Mahatma Gandhi. This
has helped him greatly, and was largely responsible for making
him great. Although the masses gather round him wherever
he goes, he is really not a man of the masses. He is
an aristocrat, and has never known what poverty is;
how can he then understand the problems of our starving
millions?

Nehru's is a very complex personality. As he himself has
explained in his *Autobiography*, he is English by education,
Muslim by culture and Hindu by an accident of birth. May-
be, on account of this, his words and actions appear to have
emanated from a split personality; there is always a wide gap
between his pronouncement and performance. Pronounce-
ments, being spontaneous, are generally devout, but perfor-
mances, being deliberate and calculated, are not so devout.
Naturally, in spite of his popularity, he is subjected to pointed
criticism by various parties and from different angles. His
attitude towards his critics, therefore, is not uniform but

215

Based on the historical facts on record, one may infer that it
was N.B. Khare himself who first referred to this quote which has
since then become a legend, regardless of the fact that there is no
truth to it.

55

JAWAHARLAL NEHRU CALLED SUBHAS CHANDRA BOSE A 'WAR CRIMINAL' IN A LETTER TO THE BRITISH PM

INDIA'S FIRST PRIME MINISTER has been defamed in myriad ways. One such theme over which Jawaharlal Nehru is constantly denigrated is his supposed relationship with Subhas Chandra Bose. Did Jawaharlal Nehru ever refer to Bose as a war criminal? Apparently so, if one were to go by a 'letter' which has been circulated widely in the social media ecosystem.

Claim: Jawaharlal Nehru wrote a letter to then British PM Clement Attlee calling Subhas Chandra Bose a 'war criminal'.

The letter is supposed to have been dictated by Nehru and was addressed to the then prime minister of Britain. In this letter, Nehru alludes to the supposed presence of Netaji Subhas Chandra Bose in Russia, months after reports emerged that he had died in a plane crash in Taiwan in August 1945.

> "Mr. Clement Attle
> Prime Minister of England,
> 10, Downing Street,
> London.
>
> 27th December, 1945.
>
> Dear Mr. Attle,
>
> I understand from reliable source that Subhas chandra Bose, your war criminal, has been allowed to enter Russian territory by Stalin. This is a clear treachery and betrayal of faith by the Russians as Russia has been an ally of the British-Americans, which she should not have done. Please take note of it and do what you consider proper and fit.
>
> Yours sincerely,
> Jawaharlal Nehru."

As can be seen above, this 'letter' is replete with spelling and grammatical errors, and makes one wonder whether a person of Nehru's calibre would have dictated a letter like this.

Fact: Apart from the fact that the letter is full of spelling and grammatical errors, an important point to be noted is that the date of the letter is 27 December 1945, whereas the official account states that Bose died on 18 August 1945.

A facsimile of this letter does make an appearance in the files related to the disappearance of Subhas Chandra Bose, which were declassified by the central government in 2016.

The letter forms part of the testimony of one Shyamlal Jain, who had deposed before the G.D. Khosla Commission established to probe the mysterious disappearance of Bose. Jain, in his testimony, had claimed that the letter was dictated to him by Nehru on the night of either 26 or 27 December 1945 at the residence of Asaf Ali, a Congress leader, in Delhi.

(7)

"After handing over the said paper to me for typing, Shri Jawaharlal Nehru went to Mr. Asaf Ali and remained busy in conversation with him for 10-15 minutes. --- I could not complete the work, because the name of the writer on that letter was not readable, and I kept waiting for Shri Jawaharlal Nehru to come and tell the name. In the meantime I went through the letter several times and this is all that I could remember to the present day. Shri Jawaharlal Nehru could not discern the name of the writer and asked me to pull out the papers and hand them over to him as they were.

"I solemnly affirm and state on oath that thereafter Shri Jawahar Lal Nehru gave me four papers from his writing pad to make on the typewriter four copies of a letter, which he would dictate to me on typewriter with which I also complied. The contents of the letter as far as I could remember were as follows:

"To   Mr. Clement Attlee, Prime Minister of   Britain
10   Downing Street, London.

Dear Mr. Attlee,

I understand from a reliable source that Subhas Chandra Bose, your war criminal, has been allowed to enter Russian territory by Stalin. This is clear treachery and a betrayal of faith by the Russians. As Russia has been an ally of the British-Americans, it should not have been done. Please take note of it and do what you consider proper and fit.

Yours sincerely,
Jawaharlal Nehru"

A perusal of historical records by Alt News has established that Jawaharlal Nehru was not even in Delhi on the dates in question. He was in Patna on 25 December and later went to Allahabad where he spent the next few days. As for Asaf Ali, he was in Bombay on 25 and 26 December 1945. Information about the whereabouts of Nehru and Asaf Ali was accessed through reports of *The Indian Express*. Moreover, a perusal of the writings of Nehru revealed that 26 December 1945 onwards, Jawaharlal Nehru was in Allahabad, from where he wrote the preface to *The Discovery of India*, on 29 December.

It is inconceivable that the letter would have been dictated in Delhi on the days on which neither Nehru nor Asaf Ali were present there. Jain's testimony was eventually not accepted by the Khosla Commission, which concluded that Netaji had indeed died in the air crash in Taiwan in August 1945.

56

NEHRU THRASHED BY MOB AFTER FAILURE IN SINO-INDIAN WAR OF 1962

Claim: Jawaharlal Nehru was thrashed by a mob after India's failure in the Sino-Indian war of 1962. To bolster this claim, a photograph of India's first prime minister was circulated widely by Nehru-baiters on social media. It showed Nehru being held from the back, amidst a crowd. Another narrative that has accompanied this image is that it was clicked in 1946, when Nehru was barred from entering Kashmir as he did not have a visa!

Messages such as these are illustrative of the constant vilification campaign against Nehru. A major theme in this regard is his failures, real or perceived. Nehru has been roundly criticized by historians and scholars over his handling of the Sino-Indian conflict of 1962 and it is thus no surprise that his detractors on social media choose to focus on this issue. In the process, unrelated photographs come in handy.

Fact: The photograph was clicked in 1962 but was unrelated to the war. It was clicked before the war.

Alt News cropped out the text from the image, reverse-searched it on Google and found that it was published by *Outlook* in 2014. The photograph was captioned, 'Braced for the worst: Nehru is prevented from plunging into a riotous crowd in 1962, before the war'. The picture was attributed to AP (Associated Press).

Searching the archives of AP with the keywords 'Nehru 1962', we found that the picture was indeed taken that year, i.e. 1962. The narrative along with the photo was, however, something else.

AP described the image as 'A security man grabbed Indian Prime Minister Nehru to keep him from plunging into a riotous crowd at a meeting of the Congress Party in Patna, India, January 1962. Later in the year, Communist China's attack on India plunged Nehru into new troubles.'

Pandemonium had broken out at the Congress session held in January 1962 in Patna as everyone was eager to get a glimpse of Nehru. Nehru had taken it upon himself to pacify the crowd and had attempted to intervene, but was restrained by security personnel. It was at that moment that the photograph was clicked.

The other narrative used to circulate the image – 'Nehru was arrested while trying to illegally enter Kashmir without a passport' – also thus stands untrue.

57

INDIAN FOOTBALL TEAM PLAYED BAREFOOT IN OLYMPICS BECAUSE NEHRU GOVERNMENT DID NOT ALLOCATE FUNDS FOR BOOTS

THAT THE INDIAN FOOTBALL team played barefoot at the Olympic Games in 1948 is a popular story which has been recalled often by sports aficionados. This legend has been given a political twist on social media.

Claim: Skewed priorities and lack of financial support by the Nehru government compelled the Indian football team to play barefoot in the 1948 Olympics.

Two photographs were juxtaposed: one showed a football player shaking hands with his counterpart, with the claim that it was taken during the 1948 Olympics. One of the players is seen barefoot. Another photo showed Jawaharlal Nehru debarking from a plane with his pet dog.

Message along with photo: 'ऐसे थे कांग्रेस नवाबों के ठाठ' (Such was the pomp of the Congress's nawabs).

Fact: The claim is not true.

Insofar as the photos are concerned, Alt News reverse-searched the images and found them to be authentic. An article published by *Frontline* had an image where Talimeren Ao, India's first football captain, was shaking hands with G. Robert, captain of the French team, in July 1948.

Nehru's photograph was found on a website owned by The Times of India Group called Times Content. According to the website, this image was clicked around January 1961.

The Indian football team at the 1948 Olympics *had* access to boots. The schedule of the 1948 Games makes an observation that the Indians played barefoot where possible but wore boots on soft ground or in rain. Alt News accessed clippings of British press which carried an observation about how the players appeared handicapped when forced to wear boots due to rain. The players were accustomed to playing without boots and continued to do so till such time that international regulations mandated them to wear boots.

This point is further corroborated in the book *Nation at Play: A History of Sport in India* (Viking), where the author, Ronojoy

Sen, writes, 'For the Indians, playing (barefoot) against booted footballers wasn't unusual; in fact, it contributed to their on-field skills'.

Image of 1948 football team

Some players *chose* to play without boots, as they were used to it. The majority of the players in the team played barefoot in those days before international regulations made the use of boots mandatory. The social media narrative suggesting otherwise was yet another attempt to malign Jawaharlal Nehru.

58

PICTURES OF PANDIT NEHRU WITH WOMEN REVEAL HIS TRUE 'CHARACTER'

THE FIRST PRIME MINISTER of independent India was hugely popular among women, evinced by the numerous pictures clicked at the time, showing Nehru in the company of women. These photographs, which are readily available in the public domain, are circulated at regular intervals across social media platforms. The intention is to paint him as a philanderer and a womanizer, with fantastic stories woven around these images, none of which are true.

A sex CD alleged to be of Patidar leader Hardik Patel had been released in November 2017. BJP IT cell head Amit Malviya took a dig at Hardik Patel and Nehru, suggesting that they had 'common DNA'.

Claim: Affectionate pictures of Jawaharlal Nehru with women, shared with the insinuation, *'It seems Hardik has more of Nehru's DNA, contrary to what @shaktisinhgohil claimed'*. The message was said to have been tweeted by BJP IT cell head Amit Malviya (although it seems to have been deleted now), along with a collage of pictures of Jawaharlal Nehru with different women.

Amit Malviya ✓
@malviyamit

It seems Hardik has more of Nehru's DNA, contrary to what @shaktisinhgohil claimed..

8:39 AM · 15 Nov 17

Fact: Some of the photos of Nehru are with his sister and niece.

In the first picture of the collage on page 163 (top left), the woman giving Nehru a peck on his cheek in full public view is none other than his sister Vijaya Lakshmi Pandit. In 1949, Pandit was India's ambassador to the United States. In the picture, she is seen welcoming her brother on his state visit to the US.

The woman in the picture on the top right is again Vijaya Lakshmi Pandit. The picture is of the time when she was the ambassador to Russia and is being received by her brother at Delhi Airport.

In yet another picture (bottom right), Nehru is being given a peck by his niece Nayantara Sahgal on his arrival at London Airport in 1955. You can also see Sehgal's mother, Vijaya Lakshmi Pandit, who was the high commissioner to UK at that time.

In the other photographs, Nehru is seen with Edwina Mountbatten, Jacqueline Kennedy and dancer Mrinalini Sarabhai, among others. One of the photographs shows him smoking a cigarette. This too is problematic, according to his social media critics.

Reference: https://timesofindia.indiatimes.com/india/bjp-it-cell-head-in-nehru-tweet-row/articleshow/61680161.cms

MAINSTREAM
MEDIA

NEWS ORGANIZATIONS, THROUGHOUT HISTORY, have been instrumental in making information available to readers, viewers and listeners in an accurate and balanced manner. In a free society, the media has a crucial role to play. The fourth pillar of democracy is trusted by citizens to uphold the responsibility of precise and prudent reporting. Thus, it is rather concerning that there have been occasions wherein the reportage of mainstream media outlets has been called into question. Accuracy has been sacrificed at the altar of sensationalism and speed. This tendency is peculiar to, although not restricted to, television news channels.

59

POSTMORTEM REVEALS THAT KATHUA VICTIM WAS NOT RAPED

THERE WAS AN OUTPOURING of anger across the nation over the brutal rape and murder of an eight-year-old girl in Kathua, Jammu and Kashmir, and the subsequent support extended to the accused by certain sections, which included members of the ruling party. There was also a lot of misinformation that was circulated about the incident.

Claim: '*No rape of the girl in Kathua, postmortem report only talks of injuries.*' This was the front-page headline of the leading Hindi daily *Dainik Jagran* on 20 April 2018. The article claimed that the post-mortem report of the Kathua incident makes no mention of rape, stating that there could be other reasons for the injuries that the victim had suffered. The report went on to explain that scratches on the thigh could be a result of a fall and the torn hymen could be a result of activities like cycling, swimming, horse riding, etc.

The report by *Dainik Jagran* also made no mention of other injuries that also pointed to a possibility of sexual assault. This article was on the front page of *Dainik Jagran* editions in New

Delhi, Agra, Allahabad, Amritsar, Aligarh, Kathua and Jammu, among other cities. *Nai Dunia*, which is a part of the Dainik Jagran group, had also published this article.

Fact: Alt News accessed the post-mortem report of the Kathua victim. In the report, there is mention of blood on the labia, vulval lacerations, vaginal bleeding, hymen not intact and blood marks on thighs and abdomen. A subsequent written response by the board of doctors of the District Hospital at Kathua to the police clearly explained that 'injuries mentioned could be because of any form of sexual assault'.

Alt News contacted Dr Jaydip Sarkar, forensic expert who works with rape victims and sex offenders and who was part of the Nithari serial killings case investigation. In a nutshell, Dr Sarkar's observations were:

1. The injuries described in the report appear to be consistent with non-consenting/forcible act in the sexual region of the victim.
2. Post-mortem information must be seen in the context of all other facts of the case (abduction, drugging of victim, homicide, confessions of the accused etc.)
3. The information available based on the two post-mortem sheets suggest, on balance of probability, that sexual assault has taken place.

Alt News tried to contact the editor of *Dainik Jagran* but he was unavailable to comment on this issue.

References: https://www.boomlive.in/after-disappearing-act-on-its-website-dainik-jagran-revives-kathua-no-rape-story/
https://twitter.com/JagranNews/status/987321568324980736

60

AMU STUDENT REPORTED AS MISSING AFTER JOINING TERRORIST GROUP

Claim: Roommate of Aligarh Muslim University (AMU) PhD student who joined Hizbul Mujahideen goes missing.

In January 2018, *The Times of India* published an article titled, 'Roommate of AMU PhD student who joined Hizbul also missing'. A day after the news broke out that PhD scholar at Aligarh Muslim University, Mannan Bashir Wani, had allegedly joined the terrorist group Hijbul Mujahideen, the paper reported that his roommate too has been missing. Quoting Aligarh Superintendent of Police (SSP) Rajesh Pandey, the paper claimed that a preliminary inquiry has revealed that the roommate who was also from Baramulla, Kashmir, was missing since July 2017.

Fact: It was a false report.

In a call to *Free Press Kashmir*, the gentleman in question stated, 'I am very disturbed since I saw this report. I have a career and a life here and this news report has put me in danger. This journalist never called or spoke to me before doing this report. I don't know how they are claiming that I am missing and what they mean by it.' This was also confirmed by the Baramulla police via a tweet.

61

PRESIDENT RAM NATH KOVIND GAINS THREE MILLION TWITTER FOLLOWERS IN ONE HOUR

Claim: After Ram Nath Kovind was sworn in as the President of India in July 2017, multiple media organizations reported that the new president had gained a whopping three million followers in the span of just one hour.

This was reported by Republic TV, *The Times of India*, Zee News, *The Economic Times*, *The Financial Express*.

Republic ✓
@republic

(Follow)   ⌄

President Kovind makes Twitter debut, gains
3 million followers in one hour

President Kovind makes Twitter debut, gains 3 million followers in one hour -...
President Kovind makes Twitter debut, gains 3 million followers in one hour
republicworld.com

2:12 PM - 25 Jul 2017

56 Retweets **162** Likes

Fact: The claim is incorrect.

Official Twitter accounts of the president, vice president and various ministries are considered digital assets that belong to the government. Twitter has a strategy for digital transition when the occupant of a position changes, to ensure continuity and preserve the digital history of the previous occupant. This was followed in the case of the @POTUS handover from former US President Obama to President Trump and the same principle was being followed for the handover of the official account of the President of India, @RashtrapatBhvn, from former President Pranab Mukherjee to President Ram Nath Kovind.

The process works as follows:

1. All tweets by former President Pranab Mukherjee are archived under @POI13.
2. The new @RashtrapatiBhvn account starts with zero tweets and all the followers from the previous account. So when President Kovind inherited the @RashtrapatiBhvn Twitter handle, he also inherited all its followers. President Mukherjee had 3+ million followers and this is the reason why it appeared that President Kovind gained 3 million followers in a matter of a few minutes.

62

MUSLIM WOMEN COME OUT IN SUPPORT OF RAM MANDIR

Claim: In November 2018, with the Ram Janmabhoomi-Babri Masjid dispute in the news, several media organizations had reported that Muslim women in Meerut had come out in support of the Ram Mandir. This was also said to have been reported by *Amar Ujala*, News18, *Patrika*, Catch News and OpIndia.

Reporting from Meerut, *Amar Ujala* published an article on 25 November titled 'We swear on God, Mandir will be built there: Muslim women come forward, men's stance unclear (translated).'

Giving the impression that members of Meerut's Muslim women community came forward in support of the Ram Mandir, *Amar Ujala* further reported – 'अयोध्या में राम मंदिर निर्माण को लेकर देश में ज़बरदस्त हलचल शुरू हो चुकी है। हिंदू संगठनों के साथ मुस्लिम महिलाओं ने भी राम मंदिर निर्माण को लेकर आवाज़ उठानी शुरू कर दी है।' (There is an immense bustle in the country regarding the issue of Ram Mandir in Ayodhya. Along with Hindu organizations, Muslim women have also begun to raise their voices vis-à-vis its construction).

News18 UP tweeted as 'breaking news' – 'Meerut: Big statement by Muslim women on the Ram Mandir construction issue. Swear on God, Mandir will be built there. Everyone's faith is attached with Shri Ram's birthplace and Muslims have nothing to do with Babri Masjid. Even Muslims were enslaved by Babur (translated).'

Fact: The reports were misleading.

What these media organizations failed to mention in their reportage was the fact that these women belonged to organizations which are affiliated to the RSS. While the names of the women spearheading the campaign were mentioned, the fact that the organizations that they worked for, 'Muslim Rashtriya Manch' and 'Rashtriya Ekta Mission', are affiliated to the RSS, was not.

63

PHOTOGRAPH OF DOCTORS PAYING LAST RESPECTS TO ATAL BIHARI VAJPAYEE

Claim: 'A photograph of the doctors paying their last respect to the veteran political stalwart has been accessed by Zee News', declared an article by Zee News following the death of former Prime Minister Atal Bihari Vajpayee on 16 August 2018.

'All the doctors stood in queue and observed silence as they bowed their heads as a mark of respect to the former Prime Minister Atal Bihari Vajpayee', said a *DNA* article, describing a picture which showed doctors standing in a row with bowed heads around a dead body on a hospital bed.

Both Zee News and *DNA* also tweeted this 'Photo of AIIMS doctors paying their last respects to Atal Bihari Vajpayee'.

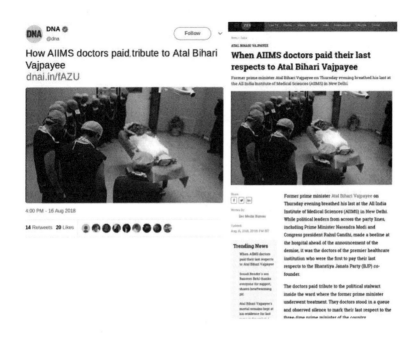

Fact: The photograph is from China.

A closer look at the photograph would suggest that it is not from India. It is a picture from 2012 of a group of Chinese doctors paying tribute to a woman whose organs were donated after her death. Medical workers bowed to seventeen-year-old Wu Huajing who donated her organs after her death in Guangdong on 22 November 2012. Both Zee News and *DNA* later deleted their tweets and revised their articles.

TARGETING
INDIVIDUALS

NOT ALL MISINFORMATION ON social media is deliberate. It is essential to make this distinction. Dissemination of information in an unintended manner is well within the realm of possibility, considering the impulsiveness associated with sharing or forwarding information.

However, there are certain entities across various platforms that are known to have actively engaged in disseminating misinformation. These are the usual suspects: pages, handles and/or accounts with a record of posting false information. These pages/accounts/groups visibly subscribe to a particular ideology or political party and post content either eulogizing their own or disparaging others'.

64

FAKE PROVOCATIVE QUOTE OF FARHAN AKHTAR

WHEN COMMUNAL VIOLENCE BROKE out in Kasganj, UP, in January 2018, a quote ascribed to actor Farhan Akhtar began circulating on social media. According to the quotation, the actor justified the death of those who were killed in the communal violence that erupted in Kasganj on Republic Day. Postcard News was among those which carried this quote.

#GauravPradhan
@DrGPradhan

Follow

This is an intellectually-challenged dimwit from Bollywood that is believed to be financed by the Mafia.

But don't worry, all RW/HRW will watch is film and make it to 100Cr club

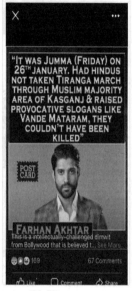

X   ...

"IT WAS JUMMA (FRIDAY) ON 26TH JANUARY. HAD HINDUS NOT TAKEN TIRANGA MARCH THROUGH MUSLIM MAJORITY AREA OF KASGANJ & RAISED PROVOCATIVE SLOGANS LIKE VANDE MATARAM, THEY COULDN'T HAVE BEEN KILLED"

POST CARD

FARHAN AKHTAR
This is a intellectually-challenged dimwit from Bollywood that is believed t... See More

169   67 Comments

Like   Comment   Share

10:07 am - 29 Jan 2018

Fact: The quote turned out to be fake and malicious. Akhtar came out with a clarification, tweeting that he had never said what is being attributed to him by nefarious elements on social media, and urged his fans and followers to be cautious about what to believe and what not to believe on social media.

Reference: https://twitter.com/FarOutAkhtar/status/958205458371 706880

65

QUOTE IN SUPPORT OF CHILD RAPISTS ATTRIBUTED TO JOURNALIST RANA AYYUB

INVESTIGATIVE JOURNALIST RANA AYYUB has repeatedly been in the crosshairs of sources of misinformation on social media. A victim of regular trolling, mostly by right-wing social media users, Ayyub has also been targeted with fake quotes. She has faced constant abuse, vilification and slander, to the extent that the United Nations' human rights body urged the Indian government to take measures to protect her from a systematic, hostile campaign.

Claim: The following quote has been attributed to Ayyub:

'Minor child rapists are also human, do they have no human rights. This Hindutva Government is bringing ordinance for death to child rapists just to hang Muslims in larger numbers. Muslims aren't safe in India anymore.'

Among those that shared this quote were an alleged parody account of the English news channel Republic TV (@republicTv) on Twitter (now suspended) and pages like *Yogi* Adityanath Ki Sena (@YogiSenaGKP) page.

Republic TV @republicTv · 7h

#BREAKING : Minor child rapists are also human, do they have no human rights. This Hindutva Government is bringing ordinance for death to child rapists just to hang muslims in larger numbers. Muslims aren't safe in India anymore. : Rana Ayyub

♡ 26   ↻ 80   ♡ 125   ⤙

Fact: The statement in question credited to Rana Ayyub is fake. The statement originated from a parody handle. In a Facebook post, Rana Ayyub clarified that she had not made any such statement and that it was from a spoof account of the news channel.

Reference: https://scroll.in/latest/877007/network-of-women-in-media-demands-immediate-end-to-online-vilification-of-journalist-rana-ayyub

66

RAVISH KUMAR CAUGHT ON VIDEO ADMITTING THAT HE WORKS FOR A POLITICAL PARTY

Claim: BJP IT cell head Amit Malviya tweeted a video of journalist Ravish Kumar in September 2017, insinuating that he was working for a political party.

In the video, Ravish Kumar makes the following statement, '*Jab tak yeh vyakti mafi nahin mangega aur mein apne party ke logo se kehta hoon ki yeh nationalist hindutva nationalist nahin hai*'. It seemed as if Kumar was speaking on behalf of a political party when he says, '*Main apne party ke logo se kehta hoon*'. Based on this, Amit Malviya tweeted, '*पत्रकार की कौन सी पार्टी होती है?*' (Does a journalist belong to a party?)

Amit Malviya ✔
@amitmalviya

Following ⌄

पत्रकार की कौन सी पार्टी होती है?

🌐 Translate Tweet

6:38 PM - 10 Sep 2017

Fact: The video clip shared by Malviya was an eleven-second excerpt from a ten-minute long speech that Kumar had given at the Press Club of India.

If one hears the complete speech, the statement that Ravish Kumar made was, 'Once he returns from China and Myanmar, the first thing he should do is to unfollow Dadhichi and acknowledge that he has made a mistake. As long as this person does not apologize, (PM Modi) should tell his party workers that he is not a Hindutva nationalist or even a nationalist. Everyone should ask this much of PM Modi by virtue of being a citizen.' (translated)

Ravish Kumar was referring to the fact that Prime Minister Narendra Modi follows Abhishek Dadhichi on Twitter. Dadhichi was accused of making insensitive comments about the late Gauri Lankesh. Kumar was in fact exhorting PM Modi to speak to his party workers. Instead, a ten-second clip was taken out of this video and circulated with an incorrect reference.

Reference: https://twitter.com/amitmalviya/status/9068669001724 92800

67

SHEHLA RASHID POCKETED THE FUNDS COLLECTED FOR KATHUA RAPE VICTIM

Claim: Shehla Rashid pocketed money crowdfunded for Kathua/ Unnao rape victims.

In November 2018, social media was brimming with allegations that Jawaharlal Nehru University (JNU) student leader Shehla Rashid had embezzled the money crowdfunded for the family of the Kathua rape victim. The allegation had floated on social media ever since crowdfunding was initiated in April 2018.

That same month, Zee News' Sudhir Chaudhary, on his show *Daily News Analysis*, had reported on the funds with the hashtag #KathuaBahanaDeshNishana (Kathua an excuse, nation the target). The broadcast was titled – 'देखें, गैंगरेप पीड़ित के नाम पर लाखों का चंदा जमा करने का खेल।' (Watch the game of collecting lakhs of funds in the name of a gangrape victim).

The slander campaign against Rashid on social media was aggressive and incessant, fuelled by Rashid's decision to deactivate her Twitter account citing 'toxicity and hate'.

Vibhor Anand @vibhor_anand · 4d   ⌄
If you donated to Shehla Rashid for the
Kathua Victim and feel cheated, then please
connect with me, I am planning to take legal
action against her. If you know anyone who
donated, please connect him/her with me.

◯ 95   ⭮ 2,373   ♡ 3,652   ⤴

Vibhor Anand @vibhor_anand · 5d   ⌄
Someone has Just suggested that a PIL must
be filed against @Shehla_Rashid for knowing
where has 40+ Lacs gone which she
collected in the name of **Kathua** Victim.If
anyone has Screenshots of her tweets of that
time, please DM me,i would initiate legal
action to recover every penny.

◯ 78   ⭮ 1,167   ♡ 2,082   ⤴

Fact: The claim is false.

On 13 April 2018, online crowdfunding platform
Crowdnewsing began the collection of funds for the family of
the Kathua rape victim with the help of Ketto. The target amount
was ₹10 lakh and Shehla Rashid was one of the initiators of
the campaign.

As public response was unexpectedly overwhelming, the
organizers decided to extend the campaign to include the Unnao
rape survivor as well. Crowdnewsing published an update on
their website on 14 April that the final amount would be equally
distributed between the two families.

On 4 November, Crowdnewsing held a press conference to elaborate on the fund collection and its subsequent transfer step by step. To counter the incessant misinformation on social media, the portal uploaded the statement of the Kathua victim's family as proof that the money was transferred.

Alt News was able to independently confirm the transfer of funds with a Jammu and Kashmir Bank official, and also with the family of the Unnao rape survivor.

Other than raising awareness about the campaign, Shehla Rashid had no role in collection or handling of the money, which was independently managed by Crowdnewsing.

References: https://twitter.com/sudhirchaudhary/status/987970226 737168384
https://twitter.com/crowdnewsing/status/1063787503864426497

FAKE POLLS,
FAKE LISTS, FAKE
ACCOUNTS

68

FAKE ACCOUNT WITH ANTI-HINDU TWEETS

Claim: '*I am waiting for 2019 when Modi loses 2019 elections. Trust me, we Muslims will make the life of Hindus Hell! We Muslims will make Hindus our slaves! Trust me, after Modi loses Muslims will rule India! [sic]*'

This was a tweet of February 2018 by a Twitter handle called @Muhammadzee69. The biography of this Twitter account claimed that the person was a teacher at Dhirubhai Ambani International school. The abusive, bigoted nature of the tweet and the alleged association of this person with Dhirubhai Ambani's school had become an object of outrage on social media. This was shared by Madhu Kishwar, Postcard News, etc.

Fact: This was a fake account created for provocation. Dhirubhai Ambani International School, Mumbai, clarified that no person named Muhammad Zeeshan had been associated with the school in any capacity or position whatsoever.

Alt News also came across a tweet by a Jammu and Kashmir-based journalist, whose photograph had been appropriated by this fake account.

The most interesting bit was the fact that this same account had earlier tweeted content which was in stark contrast to its 'anti-Hindu' tweets. There were tweets which were either abusive toward the minority community or endorsements of right-wing politics and politicians.

This was a clear case of a fake account, but clearly not the first. Sample these:

A Muslim who appreciates the greatness of Prime Minister Narendra Modi, roots for Yogi Adityanath and is critical of the Muslim community– Gini Khan, who supposedly lives in Canberra, was the toast of the right-wing social media ecosystem for her glamour and her thoroughly agreeable views.

In the aftermath of the terror attack on pilgrims at Amarnath in July 2017, a Twitter account @ShaneMalwa with the name Dr Abdul Vashisht sent out several hate-filled tweets against Hindus. Alt News had found out that the account was fake.

Zubina Ahmad, who claimed to hail from a defence background, was a favourite with right-wing social media users. Zubina's father had served in the army and her brother in the air force. Her views on most issues were stridently 'nationalist'. This account has now been suspended.

Such accounts capitalize on the tendency of social media users to outrage first and verify later, if at all. They also try to reinforce popular narratives, such as endorsement of politicians, political parties and policies.

69

BBCNEWSHUB FAKE LISTS

Claim: *'Top 10 List of Most Corrupt Political Party in the World 2018 and Rahul Gandhi led congress making it all the way to 2nd spot ... congratulations to the most corrupt political party.'*

Union Minister Giriraj Singh tweeted the above in December 2018, along with a link to a website– www.bbcnewshub.com. The website had published a 'list' of the most corrupt political parties of the world in 2018. According to this list, the Indian National Congress (INC) stood at the second spot.

This was also reportedly shared by Mohandas Pai and, Vivek Agnihotri, but seems to have been taken down now.

BBC News Hub

www.bbcnewshub.com /bbcnewshub /bbcnews

Top 10 List of Most Corrupt Political Party in the World 2018

Rank	Party Name	Country
1	Pakistan Muslim League Nawaz PML(N)	Pakistan
2	Indian National Congress ◄————	India
3	National Resistance Movement	Uganda
4	Progressive Action Party	Cuba
5	Vietnam's Communist party	Vietnam
6	Kuomintang	China
7	Nationalist Fascist Party	Italy
8	Nazi Party	Germany
9	Communist Party of China	China
10	Communist Party of the Soviet Union	Russia

Top 10 List of Most Corrupt Political Party in the World 2018

A political party is a union of people who work conjointly and struggle against one another to win political power; political parties do hire member or contenders, these parties are to run and organize elections to decide the government of any country in the world.

200

Fact: *BBCNewsHub* is an impostor website.

The website has nothing to do with the British Broadcasting Corporation (BBC). The name of the UK-based global broadcaster was used to lend credibility to this dubious website and its fake contents.

Consider the article, for instance. It is replete with grammatical errors. '...political parties do hire member or contenders, these parties are also to run and organize elections to decide the government of any country in the world [sic],' reads its first paragraph.

The ludicrous 'About Us' section of the website also gives away its falseness. It states, 'bbcnewshub.com is best place to provide complete, brief, correct, healthy and strong content for the respectable visitors which are related to all over the world. It provides the national and international current and all type of information [sic].'

70

MODI BRANDED SECOND MOST CORRUPT PM

THE WEBSITE BBCNEWSHUB IS notorious for publishing such 'lists', which include 'Top 10 most corrupt political families in the world', 'Top 10 most corrupt politicians in the world', and so on. In one such list, Prime Minister Narendra Modi was ranked second among the most corrupt prime ministers in the world.

Here is one such fake list on the right.

foxnewspoint.co

Top 10 Most Corrupt Prim

World 201

Rank	Name
1	Nawaz Sharif
2	Narendra Modi
3	Vladimir Putin
4	Shinzo Abe
5	Dmitry Medvedev
6	David Cameron

71

BBC OPINION POLL PREDICTS BJP WIN IN KARNATAKA AND RAJASTHAN

OPINION POLLS AHEAD OF elections seemingly play a significant role in shaping voter perception with regard to the position of various political parties in the fray. This is a fact that has been capitalized by purveyors of misinformation on social media, who attempt to project their own political choices as voter preferences. In the process, credibility is sought to be injected into this exercise through the use of logos and names of reputed news organizations.

Claim: Opinion poll by BBC suggests simple majority for the BJP in the upcoming assembly elections.

Ahead of the assembly election of Karnataka, a 'Janta Ki Baat' opinion poll circulated on social media predicted a win for the BJP with 135 seats out of 224. A logo of BBC News was attached to the infographic.

Again, before the Rajasthan assembly elections of December 2018, another opinion poll surfaced, showing the BJP as likely to win 135 out of 200 seats to the assembly. This too was attributed to BBC.

India - BBC News
Get the latest Asian news from BBC News in Asia: breaking news, features, analysis and special reports plus audio and video from across the Asian continent.
www.bbc.com

Janta Ki Baat survey predicts huge BJP gain in Karnataka assembly elections.

★ BJP   - 135 Seats
◆ JDS   - 45 Seats.
● Congress- 35 Seats
● Others.   - 19 Seats

The latest poll survey, conducted by Janta Ki Baat with the sample size of a 10.20 lakh respondents, says BJP is crossing 135 seats in Karnataka, a jump of 95 seats compared to the previous assembly elections. **This means, the BJP would end up as the single largest party with a clear Majority over the Congress.** The survey says that the BJP could get anything in between 125-135 seats. **PM Modi, Amit Shah ,Yogi Adityanath and former Karnataka CM Yeddyurappa are campaigning relentlessly for BJP in the state.**

Fact: These are fake surveys. BBC responded to the controversy via a tweet clarifying that the channel is not in the business of conducting opinion polls. In the case of Karnataka, an opinion poll conducted by an organization called 'Jan Ki Baat' was tweaked and changed to 'Janta Ki Baat' before it was shared on multiple platforms, including WhatsApp.

72

PARODY ACCOUNTS OF POPULAR NEWS SITES FOOL SOCIAL MEDIA USERS

PSYCHOLOGISTS HAVE LONG ARGUED that people are wired to believe what they want to. Parody accounts of news websites have figured this out and are preying upon this weakness. Even the most outrageous information tweeted by these parody handles is finding an audience, as scores of people fall for it because the information is in line with their inherent biases.

PARODY HANDLES:

1. CNN News18

The twitter handle of the now-suspended *@CNNNews18* looked almost identical to the original (@CNN) as many couldn't figure out that the letter 'I' had been used instead of the number '1' in its name. Prominent right-wing accounts have fallen victim to the tweets of this fake handle. A tweet that announced wedding bells for Congress MP Shashi Tharoor and Pakistani journalist Mehr Tarar saw many right-wing Twitterati falling over each other to retweet and comment on it. They found this 'news' so utterly believable, they missed noticing that this handle only had sixty followers. The handle was later changed to *CNN News 69*.

Abhinav Agarwal ●   ⌄
@AbhinavAgarwal

Honeymoon to be in room number 345 of the Leela Palace hotel in Chanakyapuri, New Delhi, I suppose?

@CNNnewsl8 @CNNewsl8

#Breaking : Wedding bells for #ShashiTharoor all set to marry #MehrTarar in Dubai. -Sources

10:23 PM · 11 Aug 18

2. India Tooday

When you are inclined to believe something, it is easy to overlook the extra 'o' in the account that is impersonating *India Today*. The tweet also had grammatical mistakes that were missed by those who shared it, believing it to be true.

3. Times HOW

Of all Twitter handles, Times HOW has managed to fox social media users the most. A parody handle of the popular news channel Times Now, Times HOW has snared Madhu Kishwar and Mohandas Pai.

Mohandas Pai ✔
@TVMohandasPai

Ha ha what a joke! What a juvenile! Will the Green Brigade, the JNU environmentalists pl protest at cutting trees for paper?

TIMES HOW @TiimesHow

Just In : "If Pakistan can use Ballot Papers for it's Elections, why can't India ? Using Ballot Papers instead of EVM...

5:04 PM · 25 Jul 18 from East Region, Singapore

It has also managed to deceive media organizations. In February 2018, Aaj Tak broadcast a prime-time show on a tweet by this parody handle. In another instance, Janta Ka Reporter had published an article based on a satirical tweet.

Reference: https://twitter.com/CNNViews18/status/102814652261 6000512

73

HARSH VARDHAN: STEPHEN HAWKING SAID VEDAS THEORY SUPERIOR TO EINSTEIN'S

THE BJP-LED CENTRAL GOVERNMENT'S relentless attempts to glorify ancient India is well-known. Many prominent members of the party who hold significant positions have made a slew of statements seeking to emphasize the supposed supremacy of ancient India in the realms of science and technology. In doing so, they have made statements ranging from plain inaccurate to downright bizarre.

Claim: The *Vedas* may have a theory which is superior to Albert Einstein's theory of relativity.

These are the words of Union Minister for Science and Technology Dr Harsh Vardhan. He made this rather curious claim at the inaugural session of the 105th Indian Science Congress at Imphal on 16 March 2018.

'Each and every custom and ritual of Hindus is steeped in science and every modern Indian achievement is in fact a continuation of our ancient India's scientific achievements.

We recently lost a renowned scientist, renowned cosmologist Stephen Hawking. He also emphatically said on record that our Vedas might have a theory which is superior to Einstein's theory of $E=mc^2$.

Fact: Stephen Hawking had never said that the Vedas may contain a theory superior to $E=mc^2$

Alt News found no reference to the Vedas on the official website of Stephen Hawking.

This theory that the Vedas could be the repository of knowledge superior to Einstein's theory of relativity is not new and has been floating in the public domain for some time now.

In order to fact-check the claim, Alt News searched for all the claims prior to 2011 about Hawking, Einstein and $E=mc^2$ and the Facebook page of one *hari.scientist* showed up as the original source. The page masquerades as an official page of Stephen Hawking but the handle of the page, *@hari.scientist*, clearly indicates that it is not Professor Hawking's official page. This was clarified by the admin of the page himself in a post.

The Facebook post by this page masquerading as Stephen Hawking refers to the work by Dr Sakamuri Sivaram Babu while claiming that 'Vedas might have a superior theory to Einstein's $E=mc^2$'. It is the source of this misinformation which has been shared by several social media users over the past few years.

Reference: https://www.indiatoday.in/fyi/story/science-minister-harsh-vardhan-may-have-been-a-victim-of-fake-social-media-info-1191469-2018-03-17

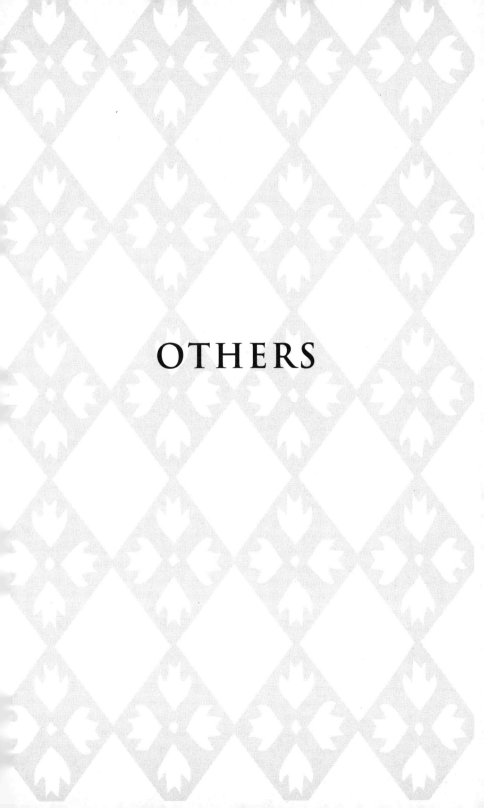

OTHERS

74

VIDEO OF HOUSES BURNT BY INDIAN ARMY IN KASHMIR

Claim: Indian army resorted to arson in Kashmir.

A statement translated from Urdu mentioned, 'Indian army starts burning down houses of Kashmiris of Bandipora, if you cannot raise your voice against this oppression or in favour of the oppressed then quit using Facebook.'

A video of homes ablaze went viral among Pakistani social media users, who claimed that this was the handiwork of the Indian army in Kashmir. It was viewed more than 1.6 million times alone from a single account on Facebook. The post claimed that Indian army personnel had resorted to arson at Bandipora, Kashmir. Thousands of social media users had shared the video on their individual timelines.

Fact: The video is of an accidental fire.

A few comments by Kashmiris on these posts claimed that the video is not from Bandipora but from Uri.

Based on this comment, we searched YouTube for incidents of accidental fire in Uri and came across a video with the title,

'Four residential houses were gutted in a massive fire incident at Lachipora, Uri'. This video was the same as the one viral on social media, but rotated by ninety degrees and in higher definition.

To further confirm the veractiy of our findings, Alt News contacted Peerzada Waseem, a photojournalist from Jammu and Kashmir, to check if the visuals are familiar to him. Waseem could identify the incident and visuals. He informed us that he had clicked pictures of the same, which were posted on Rising Kashmir's social media account.

Media reports confirmed that in March 2018, four residential houses were destroyed in a massive fire that erupted in Lachipora (Uri) area of Baramulla district in Kashmir. The fire first broke out in a cowshed and later spread to the houses in the vicinity.

Reference: https://www.youtube.com/watch?v=DEcxXFEs_MM

75

NEWSPAPER HEADLINE: MODI, XI 'MATE' 6 TIMES IN 24 HOURS

Claim: Image of a *The Times of India* article on PM Narendra Modi and Chinese President Xi Jingping with the headline: 'Modi, Xi will mate 6 times in 24 hours'.

Yes, you read that right. This was supposedly the headline of an article which appeared in the newspaper in April 2018. PM Modi had travelled to Wuhan, China, for an informal two-day summit. Former IPS officer Sanjiv Bhatt also shared it.

Fact: The newspaper clipping was Photoshopped.

The headline of the article was tampered with. Consider the image posted on the facing page. Look at how the letters 't' and 'e' in the word 'mate' are different from 't' and 'e' in the word 'times'. The 't' is longer and 'e' is bigger in the word 'mate'. Also, there are visible changes in the texture when the image is zoomed.

Modi, Xi will meet 6 times in 24 hours

Sachin.Parashar
@timesgroup.com

Wuhan: As the expansive highway from the airport leads up to a swish city centre dotted by shiny skyscrapers, it's difficult not to be impressed by Wuhan, a 10-million plus city in central China, where President Xi Jinping has chosen to host PM Narendra Modi.

It's here that Xi and Modi will have six meetings in 24 hours, including one in a boat, to discuss bilateral and global issues from, as Modi said in his departure statement, a strategic and long term perspective and respective visions and priorities. Modi and Xi will not have only one-on-one meetings. The two will have at least two meetings in which both will be accompanied by a

Modi, Xi will mate 6 times in 24 hours

Sachin.Parashar
@timesgroup.com

Wuhan: As the expansive highway from the airport leads up to a swish city centre dotted by shiny skyscrapers, it's difficult not to be impressed by Wuhan, a 10-million plus city in central China, where President Xi Jinping has chosen to host PM Narendra Modi.

It's here that Xi and Modi will have six meetings in 24 hours, including one in a boat, to discuss bilateral and global issues from, as Modi said in his departure statement, a strategic and long term perspective and respective visions and priorities. Modi and Xi will not have only one-on-one meetings. The two will have at least two meetings in which both will be accompanied by a six-member delegation.

The original headline reads, 'Modi, Xi will **meet** 6 times in 24 hours'. *The Times of India* later put out a tweet clarifying the same.

76

WHATSAPP RUMOURS AND LYNCHING

THE MONTHS OF MAY and June 2018 were ominous insofar as the sinister impact of misinformation is concerned. Rumours of child abductors abounded in various states, shared via WhatsApp. The suspicion, mistrust and fear created by these messages, which were mostly circulated along with gory images and videos of alleged child kidnappers being assaulted by the public, resulted in the death of more than twenty people across the country.

CHILD ABDUCTION RUMOURS TURN FATAL

A spate of rumours erupted in June in many states across the country, from Uttar Pradesh to Maharashtra to Tamil Nadu. These rumours were generated and spread via WhatsApp and warned citizens of child abduction gangs on the prowl.

Alt News had found that the same set of images was being used across the country. Most of the photographs were unrelated and had nothing to do with child abduction. Yet, these rumours continued unabated and spread to other states. In Maharashtra, WhatsApp messages warned of gangs who had abducted young girls and extracted their organs. These rumours resulted in a spate of mob lynchings.

A video was also widely circulated in which a child can be seen being abducted. This video was shared in different states, claiming that the gang seen in the video was active in the area.

Alt News found out that this was an old video from 2016 made for awareness purposes by an organization named Roshni Helpline. The video ends with the text: 'Every year, over 3,000 children go missing in Karachi, Pakistan. Keep an eye on your child.' The abduction was staged to educate people about rampant child abduction in Karachi.

RUMOURS FOLLOWED A LOCALIZED PATTERN

Alt News had observed that the child-abduction rumours were localized from state to state. For example, if the rumour was aimed at Maharashtra, then the message was circulated in Marathi and referred to a place in the state claiming that the child kidnappers were on the prowl in the said place. Similarly, when the messages were circulated in Gujarat, they were circulated in Gujarati and referred to a place in Gujarat. This was atypical behaviour as far as misinformation is concerned. In most cases of misinformation, the central narrative remains the same and does not change during its life cycle.

RUMOURS TAKE COMMUNAL TURN

In August 2018, the rumours of child abduction took a communal turn when messages began to circulate of a gang of Rohingya Muslims in Indore out to abduct children. This was the first instance of communalization of these rumours.

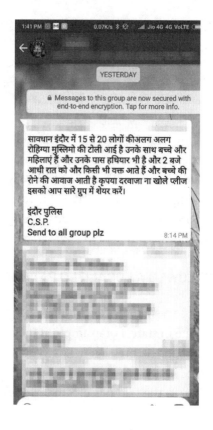

SCIENCE

77

MEASLES-RUBELLA (MR) 'MIS-INFODEMIC': ANTI-VACCINE RUMOURS

THE GOVERNMENT OF INDIA, in collaboration with UNICEF, have initiated a vaccination drive for measles-rubella (MR) vaccine. There have been several social media rumours circulated against this vaccine, particularly on WhatsApp suggesting that it contains anti-fertility agents to sterilise their children, or worse, can cause their deaths.

These rumours resurged recently when 4 four deaths were reported[15] in Gujarat, 30 to 115 hours after vaccination, in addition to 14 similar incidents of children's death in 21 states where the MR vaccination drive was carried.

Measles[16] is a severe disease, often complicated by middle-ear infection or bronchopneumonia. It can be a major cause of illness such as encephalitis (brain inflammation in 1/2,000 reported cases) that can lead to permanent brain damage and death (1/3,000 cases) due to respiratory and neurological problems.

Rubella[17] virus is transmitted by the respiratory route. In the blood, its presence occurs 5-7 days after exposure and then spreads to different organs. Symptoms can be transient rash, joint pain and arthritis. Infection in early pregnancy leads to congenital rubella syndrome (CRS) which may result in multiple fetal defects in up to 90% of cases, affecting many organs which often results in miscarriage or stillbirth.

Claim: '*Dear brothers and sisters assalamualikum all the schools have decided to give an injection for your childrens all over india so dear brothers dont let your children's get that injection object that in your child's school it's an RSS plan in which your children when they will turn around 40 they wont be able to have thier kid one teacher in kerla have told taht this injection should put to Muslim children's only so kindly do not let them get this injection for your children's safety.*' [sic]

This is a sample text in the message that was reportedly circulated.

Fact-check

The measles-rubella (MR) vaccine: The virus in the MR vaccine is live but with reduced virulence (attenuated) and is harmless in healthy humans. In addition to the weakened viruses, these vaccines may also contain ingredients required during the manufacturing and production[18] such as emulsifiers, stabilizers, preservatives and adjuvants which have been deemed as completely safe by regulatory bodies such WHO.

The efficacy of MR vaccines: From studies conducted in American schools with highest rates of vaccination[19], one dose of MR administered at ≥12 months was approximately 94% effective; where two doses were ≥99% effective, in preventing measles.

The rumours: Any vaccines, like any other medications, can have side effects but getting the vaccine is much safer than getting measles or rubella.

Infertility: Most people who get MR vaccine do not have any serious and long-term problems with it. Contrary to the claim in the rumour above, there is **no known link between the MR vaccine and mass-sterilization.**

Autism: There is no evidence that the MR vaccine can cause autism. Several studies have reported and published as primary data as well as in the form of systematic reviews of other published data.[20] Also, the original research article by Wakefield claiming this cause-effect relationship was retracted for being fraudulent which was reported by the British Medical Journal (BMJ) in 2011.[21]

The dangers of anti-vaccine rumours: Recently, the wave of anti-vaccine rumours driven diseases has taken precedence not only in India but also in North America and Europe,[22] where cases of measles (>60,000 in 2018), and deaths due to measles (72 cases) have been highest this century.

A similar anti-vaccination campaign[23], in a form of a rumour for polio vaccine, was prevalent in Nigeria in the 2003-2004, which sustained for 15 months, where, due to the lack of trust in the military, Nigerian parents did not get their children vaccinated. The rumour also suggested that the polio vaccine had antifertility agents that resulted in the subsequent boycott of the vaccine.

When MR becomes a health risk: Although MR vaccine is safe and available for every child between 9 months-15 years in the 2018 vaccination programme in India, the optimal age for MR vaccination is between 12-15 months.

However, people **should not be vaccinated**[24] if they belong in the following groups: Known allergies to MR vaccine or its components, (or antibiotic neomycin), pregnant women, patients of cancer or other diseases such as AIDS (HIV infection) that weaken the immune system, patients who have undergone radiation, immunotherapy, steroids, or chemotherapy, an immediate relative of a patient with an immune system disorder, patients of condition that bruise or bleed easily and, patients who have recently undergone transfusion of blood or received any blood products.

The side effects of MR vaccine: Some side effects of the vaccine can be a sore arm from the shot, fever, mild rash, temporary pain and stiffness in the joints.

A review of scientific literature, case studies and statistics on adverse reactions to vaccines reported that immune thrombocytopenic purpura (decreased blood platelets) and febrile seizures with fever, can be a rare side effect of MR vaccine. This decrease in blood platelets is rare (1/20,000 doses)[25] and not life-threatening. It is temporary and usually goes away without treatment. The febrile seizures are also rare (< 1 per 1,000,000 doses)[25] and are not associated with any long-term effects.

The benefits of MR vaccine: When you are vaccinating your child, you are not just protecting your child but also others in the community. Infections travel a lot faster in the community (person-person) which can lead to an epidemic. By vaccinating, you are avoiding this rapid spread by which an entire community can prevent the infection. Subsequently, you are protecting people, especially young children, from getting infected who cannot or have not vaccinated yet.

Hence, babies in large families and day-care centres are the most vulnerable and 100% community vaccination protects them via the immunity of playmates, parents or extended joint families, and this immunity is called 'herd immunity'. Contrarily, even if older children are vaccinated, younger babies will always possess a risk due to non-vaccinated individuals coming in contact with the baby.

Conclusion: Contrary to the claim in the rumour above, there is no known link between the MR vaccine and mass-sterilization in a particular religious community as the same vaccine is given to other religious communities.

Factors fueling these rumours include lack of trust in the government and health care workers, timing during which autism is detected – which is around the same time as a large number of children get vaccinated, as well as the vulnerability of babies who can be prone to infections or deaths in that age group. Such infections or deaths are a correlation but not causation as the central investigation report in India in 2018[15] had identified.

Anti-vaccine rumours have the potential to fuel an epidemic, also called a '*misinfodemic*'[14] and affect several people very rapidly, the only way to protect is to immunize through vaccinations such as polio and MR while discerning false health information from the scientific truth.

78

THE ANTI-DIABETIC AYUSH DRUGS BGR-34 AND IME-9

THE MINISTRY OF AYUSH has helped develop (in collaboration with CSIR and CCRAS)[26] two Ayurvedic anti-diabetic drugs namely BGR-34[27] and AYUSH-82 (sold as IME9)[28].

BGR-34 is being manufactured by a private enterprise called Aimil Pharmaceuticals which was awarded[29] the AYUSH brand of the year in 2016 by the Union Minister of state for Agriculture Purushottam Rupala. News channels such as News24[30] and Zee 24[31] aired *exclusive* reports along with the speech by Mr Modi on DD News[32] to promote its benefits and cost-effectiveness that gave an impression of it being a miraculous drug

The central council for research in Ayurvedic sciences (CCRAS), an autonomous body of the Ministry of AYUSH promoted a second drug for diabetes called AYUSH-82 (sold as IME9).

Claim: IME9 claims to be an effective ayurvedic drug for diabetes, without any side effects, and have been developed after double blind clinical human trial studies of more than 800 patients.

Developed by India's Council of Scientific and Industrial Research (CSIR), anti-diabetic herbal composition for Type-2 diabetes mellitus (NBRMAP-DB), which is sold under the trade name BGR-34, has been claimed to be DPP-4 inhibitor -a class of drugs used to lower blood sugar in adults with Type-2 diabetes.

'BGR-34 is a natural DPP-4 (dipeptidyl peptidase 4) inhibitor with no side effects. It is the most cost-effective Ayurvedic medicine for diabetes available at Rs 5 per tablet for patients,' said KK Sharma, Managing Director, AIMIL pharmaceuticals.[29]

Senior principal scientist of NBRI, a laboratory of CSIR, Dr AKS Rawat said that 'BGR34 has been examined on animals and a scientific study has identified it safe and effective, with clinical studies demonstrating only 67% success'.[33]

Fact-check

Claim of 'scientifically proven': When searching for human clinical trials or preclinical animal models, no scientific data for the drugs named NBRMAP-DB (BGR-34) or AYUSH-82 (IME9) were found in peer reviewed journals across *Google Scholar* and *PUBMED* database. A search for patent application at the National Botanical Research Institute (NBRI)[34] and the CCRAS website[35] yielded no results for BGR-34 and AYUSH-82 respectively.

One clinical trial[36] was found registered to CTRI (Clinical Trials Registry – India) for BGR-34 in November 2016 by Dr BP Gupta of Aggarwal Dharmath Hospital society, New Delhi which showed no data of any experiments conducted or but stated that the primary outcome of this trial 'shows promising results' in a brief concluding summary.

A review article[37] was found, *without any research data*, referring to IME9 in researchgate (a social media platform for scientists) by Dr B Negi and contained no details about the journal or the date of publication.

Claim of 'lowest cost': BGR34 is promoted as a cheaper drug with a price point of Rs 5 tablet with the recommended dosage of two tablets twice a day with meals. That makes it 4 tablets a day and amounts to Rs 20 a day or Rs 600 a month. Whereas, a 50-year-old widely prescribed drug Metformin is available at the starting price[38] of Rs 0.75 per 500 mg tablet from (Aristo) with the recommended dose between 500-2500 mg per day that can cost anywhere from Rs. 22.5 to Rs. 112.5 a month.

Claim of 'no side effects': IME9 has also been associated with many consumer complaints[39]. Contrary to the popular belief that herbal medicines do not produce side effects, some of these adverse reactions due to IME9 included constipation, blood discharge in stool, and in contrast to the claim of hypoglycaemia, increased blood sugar levels an effect that can be extremely dangerous for a diabetic patient.

Another patient also reported[40] the same increase in blood sugar as a result of IME9 treatments for just 15-day period where her fasting blood glucose increased from 324 mg/dl to 460 mg/dl (normal range 70-110).

Expert Advice:

1. Ayurvedic practitioner Bhushan Patwardhan, Interdisciplinary School of Health Sciences, Savitribai Phule Pune University, Pune rejected[41] the claims of these drugs by questioning the credibility of drug development process at AYUSH which was published his review in the *Journal of Ayurveda and Integrative Medicine* in 2016.

2. Endocrinologist Dr Om Lakhani, MD, a Consultant Endocrinologist at Zydus Hospital and MD Internal Medicine (Gold Medalist), DNB (Endocrinology), he also

refuted the 'miraculous' claims of both of these anti-diabetic medications. He also commented on how the scientific basis for these medications is lacking and suggested it *may* be against the law to promote medicines and 'miracle cures' on TV, Radio or newspaper according to the *'Drugs and Magic Remedies (Objectionable Advertisements) Act, 1954'* in India.

3. Furthermore, in 2008, Saper and colleagues from Boston University tested and reported[42]mercury, and arsenic have been detected in a substantial proportion of Indian-manufactured traditional Ayurvedic medicines. Metals may be present due to the practice of rasa shastra (combining herbs with metals, minerals, and gems high levels of lead, mercury and arsenic in 1/5th of US and Indian manufactured medicines sold on the internet by testing a randomized selection of Ayurvedic drugs across 25 different websites. This research indicates that a large proportion of locally manufactured drugs can be contaminated which emphasizes a greater need for rigorous testing.

Conclusion: Based on the current scientific data, expert opinions from the field and consumer complaints, there is limited scientific evidence for the efficacy of BGR-34 and IME9 in the management of type-2 diabetes.

We may not be able to conclude that the given side effects occurred as a result of BGR34 or IME9, and not due to a random event due to the absence of proper clinical trials. However, heavy metals detected by randomized testing of Ayurvedic drugs question the safety of these drugs (expert advice.3). A rigorous double-blind placebo RCT (randomized control trial), an essential part to the drug development process, would provide more information about the efficacy, safety and toxicity of such drugs.

Thus, the lack of scientific data makes it impossible to validate the claims made vis-a-vis BGR34 or IME9 for diabetes and thus, raises questions regarding the integrity of promotions of these drugs by AYUSH, government research institutes and the Prime Minister of India.

79

DENGUE: THE EFFICACY OF PAPAYA EXTRACT AND CARIPILL

DENGUE FEVER IS AN infection caused by viruses of *Flaviviridae* family that use mosquitoes as its host organism. The mosquito (*Aedes aegypti*) gets the virus by biting an infected person, which later spreads to other healthy humans.

Every year, when there's a surge of Dengue cases, social media posts go viral which claim that papaya, papaya leaves or papaya seeds are a cure for the disease in various Asian, African and South American countries including India.

Claim: A 2012 Facebook post[43] with an image of papaya leaves has close to 9,95,000 shares since it was first posted. It claims that the juice of papaya leaves may be a miracle cure for dengue.

'It could be a miracle cure for dengue. And the best part is you can make it at home.

The juice of the humble papaya leaf has been seen to arrest the destruction of platelets that has been the cause for so many deaths this dengue season. Ayurveda researchers have found that enzymes in the papaya leaf can fight a host of viral infections, not just dengue, and can help regenerate platelets and white blood cells.'

Yet another post of a box of Carica papaya leaves tablet called Caripill has been recirculated on social media with the following caption:

'Caripill Tablet is primarily made from papaya leaf extract to treat dengue. It raises the platelet count in patients and aids in the recovery from the disease.'

Bangalore based pharmaceutical company Micro Labs, who are the manufacturer of Caripill, also claim[44] that the drug has been approved by the Department of AYUSH in May 2015.

The National Health Portal of India, the official government website for public health information, also stated that although there is no specific treatment for dengue, medicinal plants such as guduchi, tulasi, dried ginger and papaya prevents complications and helps to control the disease faster[45].

Previously, several media houses such as *The Hindu*[46] and *The Times of India*[47] have reported that not only the tablet of papaya leaves, but the consumption of ripe papaya juice or the consumption of papaya leaves by boiling or crushing can cure dengue by raising platelet counts in blood.

Fact-check: We found two clinical trials in PUBMED in which human studies were conducted, both in July 2016, and both in *'The Journal of Association of Physicians of India'* that correlated the effect of papaya extract with a fast recovery of dengue fever on the basis of reduced platelet count.

Claim of 'reducing platelet counts': Study 1 by Gadhwal, et al. (2016) stated[48] no specific treatment is available for dengue fever induced thrombocytopenia. In few countries (Pakistan, Malaysia, Sri Lanka and other Asian countries that 'papaya leaf extract capsule raised the platelet count by 3rd day with decreased requirement of platelet transfusion.'

However, we reanalysed and plotted the data given in the article result section, we found serious interpretation problems in this study.

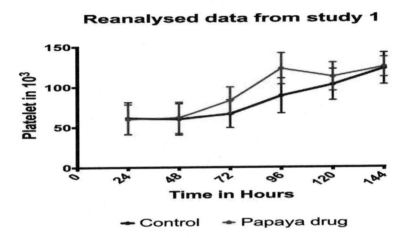

As shown in the graph, no statistically significant differences can be observed between patients receiving papaya drug vs. control group except on most days. On the day with largest differences between control and papaya group (96 hr), the standard error of the mean (shown as error bars) overlap each other. In a large sample size (n = 400 dengue patients) such as this, it can be concluded that the treatment effects are very weak.

Most importantly, the study was not blinded, which means that expectations of drug performance from the patients and health practitioners can hugely impact the results. Hence, the change in some cases can be attributed to a belief in drug efficacy.

Study 2 by Kasture, et al. (2016), however, was conducted[49] using double blinded methods, which means that drug expectations may not have impacted the result. These results were similar to study 1, where at 96 hr time point post drug administration, platelet count shows signs of recovery with papaya drug. However, error bars (variation from the average) overlap at all time points suggesting a very weak effect.

Also, in both cases, the error bars suggested that both studies may have some (not all) patients who had significantly faster platelet recovery with papaya drug, but a large majority didn't.

Claim of 'no side effects': The statement by the ministry of AYUSH and study 1, both claim there are no side effects with the papaya extract drug Caripill. But while carefully reading study 1, it quotes other observations that suggests, while a dose up to 0.25 g to 0.5 g/kg body weight is considered safe, higher doses can lead to side effects such as rash, itching, pain abdomen, nausea and vomiting. These side effects are the very debilitating side effects of dengue fever that patients are trying to recover from.

Claim that reduced platelet count can treat dengue infection and expert advice: Dr Hiten Kareliya, an infectious disease expert, suggested that 'dengue acts by penetrating deep into the tissues including the bone marrow (site of platelet production), where, through a mechanism of immune compliment activation, platelet counts are reduced. It only becomes crucial to raise platelet count when they are hazardously low (through transfusion). However, that does not mean the recovery is attained from the viral infection.'

This suggests that while every patient requires monitoring of platelets, it is not required of every dengue patient to undergo therapy to counteract reduced platelets. And doing so, does not mean one is treating the dengue infection itself.

Dr Kareliya further added, 'Change in platelet count is an indicator of immune function. There can be patients with weak or suppressed immunity, such as very young or old patients, with a dengue infection but with no major change in platelet counts, hence, the Caripill papaya drug may have a weak effect on platelet counts, but that does not reduce the viral infection itself.'

This suggests that the dengue virus works in reducing the platelet count according to the immune response of the individual. For immuno-compromised individuals, the dengue infection might persist without any major changes in blood tests. It also means that in a large number of patients, low platelets may not be an indicator of infection but dengue viral load is.

Also, he stated, 'From the total number of patients visiting his clinic due to an existing dengue infection, about 20-30% of the patients are already consuming the drug.'

This means that these patients have existing uncured dengue infection as well as symptoms of dengue despite consuming Caripill drug.

Conclusion: As the immune system of each individual is different, the drop of platelet count can vary accordingly. Therefore, varying platelet counts should be normalized as percentage change from the baseline to show robust changes across cohort. Additionally, weak effects, studies lacking patient blinding to the drug, as well as dubious statistics in the experiment suggests that the it needs more research in different conditions to conclude Caripill as an effective drug to increase platelets.

A normal recovery pattern of dengue infection (clinical course) has the same timeline as the two studies showing papaya drug and control groups. Also, there is no mention of what the loss or gain of platelets means for clinical symptoms within the first 8-10 days of dengue infection, which means the studies do not show if the symptoms such as fever or pain are reduced due to Caripill. Also, there is no data in the two studies that suggests that the viral load of dengue virus is reduced due to the papaya drug, which is the real indicator of drug efficacy.

Hence, it is highly likely that dengue patients are returning to normal health without any treatments as it occurs in most common viral infections. Even if Caripill has an effect on increasing platelets, it does not reflect on the recovery of the dengue symptoms or protect from getting dengue hemorrhagic fever.

80

THE ANTI-MALARIAL
DRUG AYUSH-64

MALARIA CONTINUES TO BE one of India's leading public health problems. India is among the top 15 countries that accounted for 80% of global malaria deaths in 2016. The CCRAS has developed an Ayurvedic formulation, AYUSH-64, that claims to treat malaria without side effects. The NRDC (National Research Development Corporation) had signed[50] an agreement with Dabur to market this drug in 2014.

Claim: A Facebook post of Ministry of AYUSH claimed[51] that CCRAS has developed a drug called AYUSH-64 to counter the developing drug resistance to malaria parasite and the widespread nature of the disease in India. It is claimed to be a polyherbal, non-toxic, anti-malarial drug that has been developed through extensive pharmacological, toxicological and clinical studies.

CCRAS claims to have conducted[52] several uncontrolled and controlled field trials in collaboration with the Malaria Epidemic Control Programme in the 1980's and 1995 for testing AYUSH-64. They report to have treated 3,600 and 10,000 *P.vivax* cases with this drug at Rajasthan and Assam.

Fact-check

Claim of efficacy: Study 1 was conducted[53] by Sharma et al. (1981) that concluded with the highest efficacy (80% response) of AYUSH-64 in 55 cases of malaria.

However, there were several major inadequacies in their study:

- *Lack of controls and standards*: The treatment response was not compared with any standard anti-malarial drug or a placebo drug. There was no mention of whether it was randomized or blinded, which makes us believe that it was neither.
- *Effect studied for a short duration*: The drug's response was followed up for only three, six or nine days. Additionally, the patients who responded after three or six days were never followed up later. Since relapse is common in malaria, it is possible that some patients may have shown resurgence of the infection after initial clearance. However, such cases would have been misinterpreted here as 'cured'.
- *Unaccounted parasite counts*: The parasite counts were not measured and accounted for analysis. Hence, there could be highly variable initial parasite counts among the patients, which could have directly affected their response.
- *Longer response time in mixed infections*: Many of the patients with mixed infections of the two strains (*P.vivax* and *P.falciparum*) showed a much longer response time of up to nine days with the AYUSH-64 drug.

This study does not meet the current standards of clinical trials on drugs. Additionally, as the susceptibility of the parasite keeps changing, this study is outdated and is irrelevant as a proof of efficacy.

Study 2: The current director of NIMR (National Institute of Malaria Research), Dr Neena Valecha, researched and published[54] her findings on AYUSH-64 in a peer-reviewed journal, Current Science in 2000.

Contradictory to the CCRAS study, in a more structured and comparative study, Valecha demonstrated that AYUSH-64 was not a promising primary anti-malarial drug. In this phase II randomised controlled trial, the patients were followed up for 28 days. The cure rate with AYUSH-64 was found to be less that 50% as compared to 100% with the standard drug. Considering poor efficacy of the drug and risk of complications, the authors had even suggested against its testing for the more severe *P.falciparum* species. The National Clinical Trials Registry of India (established in 2007) also yielded no results for AYUSH-64 implying that no recent trial has been initiated or conducted for the drug.

Conclusion: AYUSH-64, developed by CCRAS, is going to be marketed by Dabur India Ltd, as an effective anti-malarial drug. However, there are limited scientific studies which have tested the efficacy of the drug. The existing studies have major limitations like lack of controls, inadequate follow up time, low sample size and lack of normalization of baseline parasite levels, that had led to lack of credibility in the drug. Moreover, the existing studies are published by CCRAS in their self-owned low-impact journals, further questioning their credibility. In contradiction, the independent study published in a reputed scientific journal, opposes the evidence of efficacy proposed by the CCRAS. Also, malaria is commonly caused by two different parasite species, but this drug's response has been studied mainly with one species (*P.vivax*).

Consuming such medicines with very low and limited efficacy, would not only be ineffective in large populations but further burden the public health system. The disease if not completely cured can show increased relapse, resistance and continued transmission of the parasite. Further, malaria eradication program in India may get stalled if such medicines are brought into market under a popular brand like Dabur.

[1]Footnote on contribution

---

1 The above article on AYUSH-64 was produced in collaboration with D. Shivani Mittal a geneticist who researches hypoxia-mediated molecular regulation in cancer.

81

THE NON-SCIENCE OF HOMEOPATHY TREATMENTS

SAMUEL HAHNEMANN, BORN ON the 10 April 1755 in Meissen, a small town in Eastern Germany was the father of homeopathy whose ideas have been documented, referred to and practiced upon widely by the world's homeopathic practitioners. He has written close to 110 books but the *Organon of Medicine* remains one of his most popular work.

Homeopathy is one of the key branches of the Ministry of AYUSH (Ayurveda, Yoga, Unani, Siddha and Homeopathy) in the government of India, which is an ancillary health ministry that promotes the indigenous therapies of India. The Ministry of AYUSH hosts the Central Council for Research in Homeopathy (CCRH), that has completed 40 years of establishment suggesting that, in India, the promotion of homeopathy, goes beyond the conception of the AYUSH ministry in 2014.

Claim: Despite its non-Indian origins, several leading politicians along with CCRH and AYUSH have repeatedly asserted homeopathy as an effective and legitimate form of medical treatment for chronic diseases such as depression[10], autism[55], cancer[56] and diabetes[57]. The claims are elaborate, such as 'eliminates root causes of chronic illnesses where evidence-based medicine have failed', 'works without side effects' and is 'cost effective as compared to exorbitant costs associated with the private healthcare in India'. Even when during the Nipah virus epidemic, homeopaths in India (unverified by AYUSH), circulated[58] a dangerous and false rumour that 'Gelsemium 200', a homeopathic drug, can protect you from the Nipah infection – which has only been discovered since the 1990s.

Works with unknown sub-molecular mechanisms: The claims have been published in several journals by homeopaths that hypothesize that it works using 'unknown' mechanisms as below:

As claimed[59] by Hjelvik and Mørenskog (1997) in *The principles of homeopathy*, 'Homoeopathic medicines are likely to work through the body's own curative powers in a way that is best explained by comparison with vaccination. Both the homoeopathic medicine and the vaccine constitute a mild stimulus that causes mobilization of the body's defence mechanisms and thus increased ability to oppose a pathogenic influence. The homoeopathic medicine does not work at molecular level, but probably through non-materialistic qualities (possibly electromagnetic in nature) in the organism, which are so sensitive that even a mild stimulus is enough to cause a reaction. This means that homoeopathic preparations can still have an effect even when diluted beyond Avogadro's number.'

Water and its memory: Much later, around 1988, Jacques Benveniste, a French immunologist attempted to validate[60] the claims made for highly diluted homeopathic medicines by explaining that water molecules retained a memory of the antibodies that they had been in contact with before, such that a biological effect remained when the antibodies were no longer present in the system. Nevertheless, it could not be examined through evidence in the laboratory or replicated. In a landmark edition, the then 'Nature' editor John Maddox, published an editorial comment "When to believe the unbelievable" where he concluded[61] that "There is no objective explanation of these observations." The theory remained popular as the homeopaths could use it to explain many of its unexplainable mechanisms.

None of the homeopaths have 'proven' exactly how these pills work. A large number of medical researchers have concluded that it works using a placebo mechanism that relies mainly, on drug expectations.

In order to conduct a 'fact-check' on its efficacy, one needs to review the basic principles of homeopathy through the prism of what we know about human bodies today, and the explanations given by Hahnemann and other homeopaths through which the treatment is claimed to work.

Homeopathy history and principles: Hahnemann invented homeopathy in the 18th century before the systematic pharmacological study of drug safety and efficacy existed, before the knowledge of anatomy and physiology in its present form, before microbiology and the germ theory of disease. Louis Pasteur formed the relationship between germ and disease between the year 1860 and 1864, before the invention of general anaesthesia (chloroform was discovered in 1831), or, before current aseptic techniques and their uses in surgery existed. Only about a century ago, a significant majority of soldiers died in the World War due to infections such as Spanish flu, malaria and tuberculosis.

After multiple failed experiments, Hahnemann stumbled upon *quinine containing cinchona tree bark* (discovered before 1570s) as a muscle relaxant. Later, he used it to treat malaria and developed malaria like symptoms, oblivious to the other side effects and contraindications of this drug, he developed the first law of homeopathy[62].

1. The Law of *Similia Similibus Curentur* or the Law of Similitude: drugs causing symptoms that mimic a specific disease can be used to treat diseases that causes the same symptoms.

2. The Law of Single Remedy states that a prescription shouldn't be given of more than one remedy at one point of time. If multiple treatments are given at the same time, it becomes difficult to conclude which one treated the condition.

3. The Law of Minimum Dose states that one should take the smallest dose to nudge one's vital force to start the healing process. To use too much of a remedy frequently causes an aggravation of symptoms before any improvement is seen.

4. The Law of Direction of Cure states that if a disease is left untreated it moves in the opposite direction.

5. The Law of Infinitesimal Doses Under this law, homeopathy claims that when drugs such as an extract from the *chinchona tree bark* is diluted in water or alcohol, they increase their therapeutic potential. This is conducted by a serial dilution process such that a 1:100 dilution, i.e. one mL of drug per 100 mL of water or alcohol is repeated from 6 to 30 times to produce the most potent drug. In between each such dilution process, the liquid is agitated violently- - a process that claims to activate the drug properties. By this law, the minimum amount of potent homeopathy drug in the diluted liquid will be in the ratio

of 1:100, repeated 6 times, that will yield a maximum drug content with the ratio of 1:1000000000000

This means that a batch of 10,00,00,00,00 litres of drug will contain only 1 mL of the actual drug compound, while the rest will be either water or alcohol. This diluted liquid, mostly water or alcohol is poured over small glucose balls that are to be consumed several times a day.

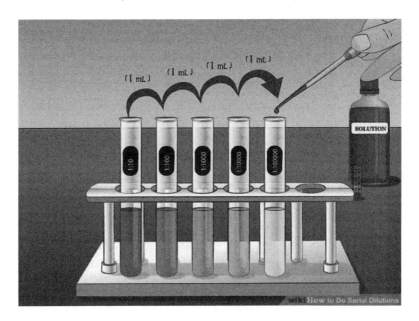

Treating symptoms not diseases: Additionally, homeopathy also has the theory of disease with three miasms, which are responsible for all human diseases and the treatments should be directed at treating these problematic miasms as a root cause:

1. Sycosis: conditions worsened by damp weather and the sea.

2. Syphilis: diseases of the nervous system such as a range of psychological illnesses such as alcoholism, depression, loss of sensations, ulcerations; the blood and skeletal disorders like heart conditions.

3. Psora: diseases of a chronic nature, all skin diseases, mental illness other than syphilitics, allergies, varicose veins, haemorrhoids, most dysfunctional diseases of organs & systems.

Fact-check

Claim of 'treating symptoms to eliminated from its roots': Each symptom is addressed using pills instead of addressing at the root cause of treatment, - which the homeopaths claim to treat. For example, pain is a symptom of many disorders such as cancer, diabetes, musculoskeletal disorders, injury or trauma. Treating the pain will not address the diabetes in a diabetic neuropathy patient as it must be dealt with treating diabetes instead. Although the symptoms of diabetes were well documented[63] in the 6th century BC by Indian healer *'Sushruta'*, the mechanisms by which occurs, such as the role of pancreas or insulin[64], were not discovered until the 19th and the 20th century respectively, which were conducted using evidence-based medicine. Hence, according to the Hahnemann's 18th century method, there may be a cure for some types of pain temporarily, as many homeopathy studies report but, unlikely for root causes of diabetes.

Claim of 'treating symptoms with minimal doses': As the understanding of human physiology and pharmacology has grown, it is increasingly getting evident that the molecular components of a cell such as proteins, ion channels, receptors have a significant role in 'mechanism of action' of drugs. Also, genes and proteins have been imaged with the highest resolution microscopes at the atomic level which have failed to reveal any non-molecular entities that support the homeopathic principles.

Importantly, the role of a minimum dosage of modern drugs to activate or bind with a certain amount of ion channels or receptors of the cell. Drugs are created specifically with respect to an optimal dosage where they are the most effective with the least of side effects. Hence, drugs that are given well below the optimal range fail to produce any effects at all. There exist no such non-materialistic or electromagnetic entities in the human bodies that allow drugs to work at such sub-molecular levels at such low quantities.

Claim of 'robust drugs devoid of side effects': Previously, most drugs were derived from natural sources, purified and extracted which later could be synthesize as molecules in the laboratory. Until now, there is no drug that is specifically designed to target a single system, but ignoring the rest of the systems. Hence, any drug that has a robust effect will have side-effects. The drugs are tested by keeping this notion in perspective that the critical effect is more beneficial and less dangerous than its given side effect.

Claims of working through parallel mechanisms from modern evidence-based drugs: As the mechanisms of drugs are unproven, there is no evidence that an entire parallel system in the human immune system exists that is unfounded by the modern immunological techniques.

Expert advice and drug expectations that incorporate a placebo effect: As Professor Edzard Ernst, a German academic physician and author of several books[65] on complementary medicine including homeopathy, stated that, homeopathic practitioners '...

live by (and from) the error of 200 years ago'. There is no evidence that homeopathy works any better than placebo treatments.

Several large trials with large patient numbers, expert opinions, systematic reviews later, it is concluded[66] in a review by Ernst in 2002 that 'the best clinical evidence for homeopathy available to date does not warrant positive recommendations for its use in clinical practice.'

An endless list of systematic reviews by several researchers, including homeopaths, have come to similar conclusions that the effects were no different than a placebo or a sugar pill. A large majority of homeopathy studies that show significant differences in efficacy as compared to placebo do not comply to the standards of research, which control for experimental, bias, comparison between drugs and placebo, statistics, double-blinding or number of patients.

International rulings on homeopathy: The Australian Government NHMRC[67], Australian National Health and Medical Research Council, after analysing over 1,800 scientific papers has concluded that homeopathy *'relies on super-diluted substances'* and has given the final verdict on the ineffectiveness of homeopathy as a treatment based on evidence based practice in a variety of clinical conditions. In essence, it concluded that there is no scientific basis for homeopathy and no quality evidence of its efficacy.

Recently, the Parliament of UK also passed[68] a regulation that homeopathy will not be prescribed as a part of the public health system (NHS). Other countries in European Union have also passed similar laws to control and regulate homeopathy practice to limit as 'patient initiated and funded last-resort treatment'.

In 2016, the Federal Trade Commission (FTC) of the US Government declared[69] that homeopathic medicines cannot claim efficacy without reliable evidence. If no evidence, exists, it must be labelled accordingly and that, these medications were based on ancient theories discarded by modern science.

Conclusion: Understanding the basic principles of homeopathy, in particular, the law of infinitesimal doses, it is clear that the medicine does not contain enough drug to treat any disorder, i.e. it either consists largely of water or alcohol, poured over sugar pills. While thoroughly researched evidence-based pharmacology suggests the optimum drug dosage in the body is a major contributing factor for drug efficacy. Therefore, according to the modern scientific explanation, these homeopathic drugs simply should not work based on a mechanism, but may work, for some, as a placebo. Since such treatments have the tendency to give a false notion of treatment, many preventative or controllable illnesses can turn into long lasting untreatable or complicated disorders.

82

DEPRESSION: THE EVIDENCE FOR ITS BIOLOGICAL ORIGIN

THE WORLD HEALTH ORGANIZATION (WHO) acknowledges that depression is the most common mental health disability. It can be as debilitating as any physical disability. Everyday actions such as going to work or even getting out of bed for the day can be an effort. It is one of the major causes of illnesses in the world that affects women (twice as much) and teenagers the most and can also lead to suicide. However, men and people of other age groups can also be affected by depression.

Symptoms include irritability, low self-esteem, feelings of hopelessness, worthlessness, and guilt, decreased ability to concentrate and think, changes in appetite, weight and sleep pattern, low energy, fatigue, or increased agitation, decreased interest in pleasurable stimuli (e.g., sex, food, social interactions), and, recurrent thoughts of death and suicide

Major misconceptions exist about depression such that it is not a real illness, anyone can get depressed, it is just 'self-pity', it can be controlled with 'positive thinking, 'depressed people are want to be lazy all the time', 'depression is just another name of sadness', and many more.

As a result, a plethora of claims and advices circulate for depression; a large number of which comes from spiritual gurus, priests and local saints, in addition to practitioners of alternative medicine practitioners. However, advices based on misinformed or lack of scientific evidence coming from the Ministry of Health, India, can be the most dangerous.

Claim: '#Depression is a state of low mood that affects a person's thought, behaviour, feeling & sense of well-being. One must take up activities that keep him or her boosted in order to cope with depression. #SwasthaBharat #MentalHealth #LetsTalk'.

The Ministry of Health and Family Welfare (MoH&FW) Twitter account posted the aforementioned text as a public awareness measure on depression. An infographic accompanied the tweet that advised a list that included 'following a routine, travelling, being creative, taking multivitamins, thinking positively, practicing yoga, staying clean, sleeping for a minimum of eight hours, eating fruits and going for a walk' as measures to help cope with depression.

The tweet also suggested that 'Depression is a state of low mood that affects a person's thought, behaviour, feeling, entrance of well-being. One must take up activities that keep him or her boosted in order to cope with depression.'

A few days later, the National Health Portal (NHP), a government body, released[70] a statement on their website elaborating on the mental health disorders, mainly: anxiety, depression and sleep disorders.

In one of the sections, they maintained that mental exercises that included 'training to 'tune' to the happenings inside and outside the body' is an effective way to deal with mental health illnesses. But, the NHP did not mention how to practice this 'tuning'. The NHP article states:

'It is also necessary that, for the mental faculties to grow, they must be constantly trained and tuned to the happenings inside and outside the body ... Be it fire or be it nanotechnology, no great invention or discovery has come without overcoming challenges and more so not without the sanity of a balanced mind. We must therefore keep facing challenges if we want our mind to remain healthy.'

The NHP article also emphasized 'food for thought'. It stated:

'As in the case of maintaining general hygiene for physical health, developing a healthy mind is through imbibing good food for thought or 'ChaitikAhaar'. This food for thought can be imbibed by participating in healthy discussions, socializing, meeting new people and meditating.'

The NHP also blamed socio-economic problems like 'poor socioeconomic state, a broken family and professional difficulties' and, added that clean and positive surroundings can help heal these problems. Lastly, they also added that homeopathy can correct these issues.

Fact-check: The more severe forms of depression cannot be treated with positive thinking or diet. The socio-economic status may be a significant correlate but may not be the sole cause of major depression. With pre-existing robust scientific evidence, it is widely accepted that a combination of: A. *Biological,* (genetic vulnerability, pubertal hormones, pubertal timing and development) factors as vulnerabilities, that interact with, B. *Environment,* (negative and adverse life events) that account for heightened rates of depression in humans.

Study on genetic causes: There are several studies that have identified various genes that have a major role in major depressive disorder (MDD), commonly known as depression.

An epidemiological study[71] on adoption and twin studies in the American Journal of Psychiatry published in 2000, concluded that while environment was significant to the cause of depression, it is reliant on genetic heritability from biological parents. The study concluded that major depression is inheritable from genes and its heritability results from genetic influences.

A study in the prestigious journal 'Science', published in 2018, suggested[72] that there is a shared genetic basis or heritability in major common disorders of the brain and this heritability (inherited from parents' genes) depended on how early the onset of the disorder started in an individual. Hence, the study concluded that genes have a huge role in not just depression, but in several other mental health disorders.

In epidemiological literature from Mayberg and colleagues[73] (2013) and, by Fava & Kendler[74] (2000), it has been concluded that about 40%–50% of the risk for depression is based on genetics. These studies make major depression a highly heritable disorder, similar to several common complex diseases such as type 2 diabetes, hypertension, and some cancers.

Similar to other psychiatric disorders and most common complex diseases, the search for specific genes for depression that confer this link has not been founded with a genetic abnormality being identified to date with certainty. The several reasons for this difficulty in finding gene specificity has been detailed[75] by Burmeister in 1999. These studies conclude that depression is much complex and several genes may involve in producing the neurobiology of depression.

Study on environmental causes: The link between stress or adverse life events and depression cannot be ignored. However, stress alone is not sufficient to cause depressive disorder. Most individuals do not get depression after severe stressful events such as physical or sexual abuse. Instead, some of those individuals get post-traumatic stress disorder (PTSD), which has a distinct course, symptoms and treatment.

Another study, published in 1999 in the American Journal of Psychiatry suggested[76] that although stressful life events have a substantial causal correlation episode of major depression, about 1/3rd of the association between stressful life events and onsets of depression is non-causal. This could be because individuals (biologically) predisposed to depression may select themselves into high-risk environments.

Hence, depression has distinct molecular physiology and genetics. A lowered emotional state such as temporary sadness (due to the environment), is not the causal factor without predisposition to inherited genes that are linked with depression.

More evidence to link biology by studying depression after childbirth: About, 13-19.8 % of women experience a mental health disorder, mainly depression, after giving birth. Postpartum depression, which starts with the onset of post childbirth hormonal changes, is clearly linked with physiological changes in the mother after birth. In a large number of those affected mothers, there are no external environmental stimuli of sadness or grief. These symptoms have been shown to be ameliorated with robust anti-depressants.

Claims on treatment: While, NHP quoted statements from WHO on mental health; WHO, nowhere suggested that mental health can be 'maintained' by 'tuning' exercises, the meaning of which is not explicitly described. Although, there is evidence that physical exercise and mindfulness can help with mild depression, in higher forms of major depressive disorders, exercise alone has not shown any robust benefits.

A statement by WHO on mental health recognizes the importance of scalable psychological interventions[77] as well as antidepressant medications (such as selective serotonin re-uptake inhibitors and tricyclic antidepressants)[78] in cases of depression. In contrast, the NHP provided no suggestions of seeking professional help similar to the statements by WHO.

While some of the options suggested by the MoH&FW can help alleviate one's low emotional state such as sadness; lifestyle choices, such as being creative, diet or travelling, cannot be categorized as effective treatments for dealing with depression.

In addition to that, there was no advices for proven & effective treatments available for clinical depression by the Ministry. The only mention related to medications was of multivitamin pills which, according to a study[79], have failed to show any efficacy in treating or in decreasing its prevalence.

The NHP's suggestion for treatment – homeopathy, is scientifically unproven to treat depression in comparison with placebo treatments. Several studies, both as individual studies[80] specifically for depression and a meta-analysis[81] of several studies, conducted on homeopathic treatments, concluded that homeopathy is ineffective for depression.

In contrast, a study published in 2018, in *The Lancet*, compared[82] efficacy of 21 antidepressant drugs, against placebo, for the acute treatment for major depressive disorder. This study by a collaborative team of psychiatrists and scientists across the UK, USA, France, Switzerland, Germany, The Netherlands and Japan concluded that all 21 antidepressants tested were more efficacious than a placebo drug.

Conclusion: The suggestions for depression by the Health ministry and, also, in the statement by the NHP indicates the extent of misinformed medical advice passed from the health advisors of the ministry to the general population. Carelessly, equating socio-economics as the only cause for mental health issues, without considering the research behind these illnesses, is grave medical negligence and lack of diligence coming from the Ministry of Health & Family Welfare, the mainstream Health Ministry in India.

The National Health Portal claims to be a portal to establish a single point access for authenticated health information for citizens, students, healthcare professionals and researchers. Its unconditional support for homeopathy while neglecting all the proven treatments available is irresponsible, misleading and indicates disregard for the evidence-based practice and the profession of medicine.

BIBLIOGRAPHY FOR THE SCIENCE
SECTION (PREFACE AND CHAPTERS)

1. World Health Organization. Ten threats to global health in 2019. *Who* (2019). Available at: https://www.who.int/emergencies/ten-threats-to-global-health-in-2019.

2. Sharon Otterman. New York Confronts Its Worst Measles Outbreak in Decades. *New York Times* **91,** 399–404 (2017).

3. Leong, W. Y. Measles cases hit record high in Europe in 2018. *Journal of Travel Medicine* **25,** (2018).

4. Gyenes, N. & Mina, A. X. How Misinfodemics Spread Disease. *The Atlantic* (2018).

5. Parikh, R. Fact-check: Dr. Dixit's 'Two meals a day' diet for weight-loss & diabetes. *Altnews* **91,** 399–404 (2018).

6. Shaikh, S. The Measles-Rubella (MR) vaccine: Myths of anti-fertility agents & vaccine related deaths. *Altnews* (2018).

7. Shaikh, S. Is Homeopathy an effective form of treatment? *Altnews* (2018).

8. Shaikh, S. Are AYUSH supported BGR-34 and IME-9 drugs safe and effective for diabetes? *Altnews* (2017).

9. Shivani Mittal. The inefficacy of AYUSH-64, the anti-malarial Ayurvedic drug developed by Ministry of AYUSH - Alt News. *www.altnews.in* (2019).

10. Shaikh, S. Depression is not 'low mood': Misleading advice from the Ministry of Health. *Altnews* (2018).

11. Norrgard Karen. Human Testing, the Eugenics Movement, and IRBs. *Nat. Educ.* **1,** 14 (2008).

12. Baron-Cohen, S. The truth about Hans Asperger's Nazi collusion. *Nature* **557,** 305–306 (2018).

13. Amy Harmon. Why White Supremacists Are Chugging Milk (and Why Geneticists Are Alarmed). *New York Times* (2018).

14. Warraich, B. H. Dr . Google Is a Liar. *New York Times* 2017–2018 (2018).

15. All India | Indo-Asian News Service. 4 Children Reportedly Dead After Measles Rubella Vaccination In Gujarat. *NDTV* (2018).

16. WHO. WHO | Measles. *WHO* (2011). Available at: https://www. who.int/biologicals/areas/vaccines/mmr/measles/en/. (Accessed: 4th March 2019)

17. WHO. WHO | Rubella (German Measles). *WHO* (2014). Available at: https://www.who.int/biologicals/vaccines/rubella/en/. (Accessed: 4th March 2019)

18. Pollard, A. Vaccine ingredients | Vaccine Knowledge. *Vaccine knowledge project* (2019). Available at: http://vk.ovg.ox.ac.uk/ vaccine-ingredients. (Accessed: 4th March 2019)

19. Sutcliffe, P. A. & Rea, E. Outbreak of measles in a highly vaccinated secondary school population. *CMAJ* **155,** 1407–13 (1996).

20. Wilson, K., Mills, E., Ross, C., McGowan, J. & Jadad, A. Association of Autistic Spectrum Disorder and the Measles, Mumps, and Rubella Vaccine. *Arch. Pediatr. Adolesc. Med.* **157,** 628 (2003).

21. Godlee, F., Smith, J. & Marcovitch, H. Wakefield's article linking MMR vaccine and autism was fraudulent. *BMJ* **342,** c7452–c7452 (2011).

22. Sarah Boseley. Measles cases at highest for 20 years in Europe, as anti-vaccine movement grows | World news | The Guardian. *Guardian* (2018).

23. Jegede, A. S. What Led to the Nigerian Boycott of the Polio Vaccination Campaign? *PLoS Med.* **4,** e73 (2007).

24. CDC. Vaccine Information Statement | MMR | Measles-Mumps-Rubella | VIS | CDC. *Centers for Disease Control and Prevention* (2018). Available at: https://www.cdc.gov/vaccines/hcp/vis/vis-statements/mmr.html. (Accessed: 4th March 2019)

25. American Academy of Family Physicians., J. P., Pawlowski, R. H. T. & Thomas, S. *American family physician. American Family Physician* **95,** (American Academy of Family Physicians, 1970).

26. CSIR India. CSIR-NBRI Introduction BGR-34 Anti Diabetic Medicine - YouTube. (2017).

27. AIMIL pharmaceuticals. Buy BGR-34 Tablet, BGR-34 Ayurvedic Diabetes Medicine Online India – AIMIL. *https://www.bgr-34.life* Available at: https://www.bgr-34.life/products/natural-treatments-of-diabetes-bgr34. (Accessed: 4th March 2019)

28. PIB. *Anti-Diabetic Drug 'Ayush-82' to be commercialised. Government of India Ministry of Science & Technology* (2016).

29. AIMIL Pharmaceuticals. AIMIL Pharmaceuticals Wins AYUSH Brand of the Year – Aimil Pharmaceuticals. *http://www.aimilpharmaceuticals.com* (2016). Available at: http://www.aimilpharmaceuticals.com/aimil-pharmaceuticals-wins-ayush-brand-of-the-year/. (Accessed: 4th March 2019)

30. News24. Scientifically validated Rs 5 anti-diabetes herbal drug launched by CSIR - YouTube. (2015).

31. ZEE 24 TAAS. Pune | Ayurvedic Medicine | BGR 34 | For Diabetics Patient - YouTube. (2016).

32. DDNews. PM Narendra Modi Ji awarded BGR-34 for CSIR Technological Awards 2016 - YouTube. (2016).

33. CRS. *BGR-34: Herbal Anti- Diabetes Drug Launched by CSIR.* (2015).

34. CSIR. National Botanical Research Institute. Available at: http://www.nbri.res.in/. (Accessed: 4th March 2019)

35. CCRAS. Central Council for Research in Ayurvedic Sciences, Ministry of AYUSH, Government of India |. Available at: http://www.ccras.nic.in/. (Accessed: 4th March 2019)

36. BP Gupta. *A clinical study of BGR 34, in patients with type 2 diabetes mellitus. Scientific Title of Study Controlled clinical study of an Ayurvedic anti diabetic formulation (BGR-34) for its efficacy and safety in patients with type 2 Diabetes mellitus.* (2017).

37. Negi, B. *From ancient medical knowledge to the modern drug development in India.* (2016).

38. Medline India - metformin. Available at: http://www.medlineindia.com/endocrine/metformin.htm. (Accessed: 4th March 2019)

39. IME 9 Complaints. *https://www.complaintboard.in* (2018). Available at: https://www.complaintboard.in/complaints-reviews/ime-9-1529967.html. (Accessed: 4th March 2019)

40. Chagala Tripathy. [Review] IME9 Ayurvedic Medicine Is a Fraud Medicine by Kudos - OxyMos. *Oxymos* (2017). Available at: http://oxymos.blogspot.com/2016/08/review-ime9-ayurvedic-medicine-is-fraud.html. (Accessed: 4th March 2019)

41. Patwardhan, B. Ayurvedic drugs in case: Claims, evidence, regulations and ethics. *J. Ayurveda Integr. Med.* **7,** 135–137 (2016).

42. Saper, R. B. *et al.* Lead, Mercury, and Arsenic in US- and Indian-Manufactured Ayurvedic Medicines Sold via the Internet. *JAMA* **300,** 915 (2008).

43. HealthDigest. Health Digest - Posts. *Facebook* (2012). Available at: https://www.facebook.com/healthdigest/photos/a.187939824672351/210685889064411/?type=3&theater. (Accessed: 4th March 2019)

44. M.Sai Gopal. New drug to increase platelet count - The Hindu. *The Hindu* (2015).

45. NHP. Ayurvedic perspective of Dengue Fever | National Health Portal of India. Available at: https://www.nhp.gov.in/ayurvedic-perspective-of-dengue-fever_mtl. (Accessed: 4th March 2019)

46. M.Sai Gopal. Can Ayurveda help dengue patients? - The Hindu. *The Hindu* (2015).

47. Ankur Tewari. Dengue scare: Ayurved gets popular as antidote in Gujarat | India News - Times of India. *The Times of India* (2015).

48. Gadhwal, A. K. *et al.* Effect of Carica papaya Leaf Extract Capsule on Platelet Count in Patients of Dengue Fever with Thrombocytopenia. *J. Assoc. Physicians India* **64,** 22–26 (2016).

49. Kasture, P. N., Nagabhushan, K. H. & Kumar, A. A Multi-centric, Double-blind, Placebo-controlled, Randomized, Prospective Study to Evaluate the Efficacy and Safety of Carica papaya Leaf Extract, as Empirical Therapy for Thrombocytopenia associated with Dengue Fever. *J. Assoc. Physicians India* **64,** 15–20 (2016).

50. Government of India & Ministry of Science & Technology. *Agreement for Commercialisation of an Ayurvedic Formulation for*

Treatment of Malaria and an Ayurvedic Formulation for Treatment of Diabetes. PIB (2016).

51. The ministry of AYUSH. CCRAS AYUSH64 – Facebook post. (2018). Available at: https://www.facebook.com/moayush/photos/a.1960540694171182/2676261769265734/?type=3&theater. (Accessed: 4th March 2019)

52. CCRAS. *Malaria Epidemic Control Programme.* (2014).

53. K.D. Sharma, M.L. Kapoor, Miss. S.P. Vaidya, P. K. S. A Clinical Trial of 'Ayush – 64' (A coded Anti-malarial Medicine) in cases of Malaria. *J. Res. Ayurveda Siddha* **2**, 309–326 (1981).

54. Valecha, N. *et al.* Comparative efficacy of Ayush-64 vs chloroquine in vivax malaria. *Curr. Sci.* **78**, 1120–1122 (2000).

55. Shaikh, S. Do the AYUSH based treatments for autism stand up to scientific scrutiny? *Altnews* (2018).

56. The Government of India, M. of A. *Year End Review 2018- Ministry of AYUSH. PIB* (2018).

57. Eswara Das. Diabetes Mellitus and Homeopathic Approach | National Health Portal of India. *NHP* (2016). Available at: https://www.nhp.gov.in/diabetes-mellitus-and-homeopathic-approach_mtl. (Accessed: 5th March 2019)

58. Sumaiya Shaikh. No, homeopathic pill Gelsemium 200 will not protect you from Nipah virus infection. *Altnews* (2018).

59. Hjelvik, M. & Mørenskog, E. The principles of homeopathy. *Tidsskr. Nor. Laegeforen.* **117**, 2497–501 (1997).

60. Poitevin, B. Jacques Benveniste: a personal tribute. *Homeopathy* **94**, 138–139 (2005).

61. John Maddox. When to believe the unbelievable. *Nature* **333**, 787–787 (1988).

62. Hahnemann, S., Boericke, W. & Dudgeon, R. E. *Organon of medicine : word index included.* (1893).

63. Lakhtakia, R. The history of diabetes mellitus. *Sultan Qaboos Univ. Med. J.* **13**, 368–70 (2013).

64. Quianzon, C. C. & Cheikh, I. History of insulin. *J. community Hosp. Intern. Med. Perspect.* **2**, (2012).

65. Ernst, E. (Edzard). *Homeopathy : the undiluted facts : including a comprehensive A-Z lexicon.*

66. Ernst, E. A systematic review of systematic reviews of homeopathy. *Br. J. Clin. Pharmacol.* **54,** 577–82 (2002).

67. The Australian Government, N. health and medical research council. *Homeopathy- NHMRC.* (2015).

68. Science and Technology Committee. House of Commons - Evidence Check 2: Homeopathy - Science and Technology Committee. *The House of Commons, The UK Parliament* Available at: https://publications.parliament.uk/pa/cm200910/cmselect/cmsctech/45/4502.htm. (Accessed: 5th March 2019)

69. FTC. *FTC Issues Enforcement Policy Statement Regarding Marketing Claims for Over-the-Counter Homeopathic Drugs | Federal Trade Commission. The US Government Federal Trade Commission* (2016).

70. NHP. Mental Health | National Health Portal Of India. *National health portal India* (2017). Available at: https://www.nhp.gov.in/healthlyliving/mental-health. (Accessed: 5th March 2019)

71. Sullivan, P. F., Neale, M. C. & Kendler, K. S. Genetic Epidemiology of Major Depression: Review and Meta-Analysis. *Am. J. Psychiatry* **157,** 1552–1562 (2000).

72. Brainstorm Consortium, T. B. *et al.* Analysis of shared heritability in common disorders of the brain. *Science* **360,** eaap8757 (2018).

73. Mayberg, H. *Neurobiology of Mental Illness.* (Oxford University Press, 2013). doi:10.1093/med/9780199934959.001.0001

74. Fava, M. & Kendler, K. S. Major depressive disorder. *Neuron* **28,** 335–41 (2000).

75. Burmeister, M. Basic concepts in the study of diseases with complex genetics. *Biol. Psychiatry* **45,** 522–32 (1999).

76. Kendler, K. S., Karkowski, L. M. & Prescott, C. A. Causal Relationship Between Stressful Life Events and the Onset of Major Depression. *Am. J. Psychiatry* **156,** 837–841 (1999).

77. WHO | Scalable psychological interventions. *WHO* (2017).

78. WHO. Depression. *WHO* (2018). Available at: https://www.who.int/news-room/fact-sheets/detail/depression. (Accessed: 5th March 2019)

79. Cho, Y. J. *et al.* Prenatal multivitamins containing folic acid do not decrease prevalence of depression among pregnant women. *J. Obstet. Gynaecol. (Lahore).* **28,** 482–484 (2008).

80. Spence, D. S. Day to day management of anxiety and depression. *Br. Homeopath. J.* **79,** 39–44 (1990).

81. The Australian Government NHMRC. *Evidence on the effectiveness of homeopathy for treating health conditions.* (2015).

82. Cipriani, A. *et al.* Comparative efficacy and acceptability of 21 antidepressant drugs for the acute treatment of adults with major depressive disorder: a systematic review and network meta-analysis. *Lancet* **391,** 1357–1366 (2018).

A NOTE ON THE CONTRIBUTORS

Pratik Sinha is the co-founder and editor of Alt News. Previously, he has worked as a software engineer in India, US and Vietnam specializing in embedded systems and wireless technologies. He's also a member of Jan Sangharsh Manch which is a civil liberties organization based in Ahmedabad.

Dr Sumaiya Shaikh is a neuroscientist based in Sweden and the editor for Alt News Science. She holds a PhD in neurophysiology from Sydney, Australia. Currently, she is studying the human brain during violent aggression as well as writing a popular book on the science behind why ordinary people commit violent crimes. She advocates for evidence based methods in science and health.

Arjun Sidharth is a writer at Alt News. He has previously worked in the television news industry, where he managed news bulletins and breaking news scenarios, apart from scripting numerous prime time television stories.

Nirjhari Sinha is the director of Pravda Media Foundation, the non-profit initiative under which Alt News functions. She ensures that the establishment runs without any hiccups and is responsible for the operations and finances of the company. She's also the current convener of Jan Sangharsh Manch, a civil liberties organization based in Ahmedabad.

Mohammed Zubair is the co-founder of Alt News and has been associated in different capacities with the initiative since its very inception. Previously, he was a technical solution manager in the telecom sector. Currently, he is responsible for research, monitoring and timely delivery of content on the Alt News platform.

Priyanka Jha, an economics graduate, started her career in the field of accounting and statistics. The research skills she honed because of her education helped her pursue a role in the domain of misinformation. She is a researcher at Alt News and manages the organization's Hindi portal.

Pooja Chaudhuri began her career working as a market research fellow. However, her deep-seated interests in media and a flair for writing led her to the field of journalism. She works in the capacity of a writer at Alt News, actively pursuing media misreports.

Jignesh Patel is a computer science graduate whose keen interest in journalism pushed him to pursue a master's degree in the field. He harbours a knack for spotting fake news and specializes in researching its source. With misinformation actively circulated via videos, Jignesh is also passionate about visual investigation.